WALKING IN SCOTLAND'S FAR NORTH

About the Author

Andy Walmsley was born in Preston, Lancashire, in 1959. From an early age mountains and wild places held a fascination for him, and early trips to Scotland began a deep affection for the unique landscapes of the Highlands.

Throughout his teens, Andy was active in various outdoor and physical activities, including cycling, caving and fellwalking, and during this time he made his first trip to the far north of Scotland, climbing Spidean Coinnich (Quinag) at the age of 14. He resolved to explore the area more fully as soon as the opportunity presented itself, and this book is the result of all his explorations from 1974 until 2002.

Despite a serious motorcycle accident in 1981, in which he lost his right arm, Andy remains an active mountain-goer. He took up the arduous sport of fell-running in 1985 and still competes in mountain events all over the British Isles.

During the late 1980s he spent time exploring the Spanish Sierra Nevada mountains, writing a guide which was published by Cicerone in 1993, and during this time he set a record of 15 hours and 5 minutes for the traverse of all the Sierra Nevada's 3000m peaks – the Integral de Los Tres Mil – which still stands today.

WALKING IN SCOTLAND'S FAR NORTH

by Andy Walmsley

CICERONE

2 POLICE SQUARE, MILNTHORPE, CUMBRIA LA7 7PY
www.cicerone.co.uk

© A. Walmsley 2003
ISBN 1 85284 377 2
A catalogue record for this book is available from the British Library.

Photographs by Harry Walmsley, unless otherwise credited.

Maps based on Ordnance Survey® material, licence number PU100012932

Acknowledgements

I must give special thanks to all the people who have assisted me with this project, either with advice, comment, and practical help or by accompanying me on the various outings. These include my daughter Andria, who braved the rain and snow to keep Dad company on more than one occasion. Tim Kelly, who drew the excellent maps used in the book, provided some photos and came along on a couple of trips to ensure that we covered the routes in double-quick time. Ian Roberts, who provided his inimitable insight into the area, sussed out a couple of routes which I wouldn't have thought of, and also took some photos. Last but not least, my uncle, Harry Walmsley, who provided the majority of the photos used in the book, which are of a much higher standard than any I could have taken.

Advice to Readers

Readers are advised that while every effort is taken by the author to ensure the accuracy of this guidebook, changes can occur which may affect the contents. It is also advisable to check locally on transport, accommodation, shops, etc.

The publisher would welcome information on any updates and changes.

Front Cover: *Loch Lurgainn and Cul Beag from Stack Polly*

CONTENTS

Introduction	13
Topography	15
Climate	18
Plants, Birds and Animals	19
Bases	20
Getting There	25
Roads within the Area	26
Using the Guide	34
Maps	34
Essential Equipment	35
Mountain Bikes	36
Gaelic and Norse Place-names	36

Assynt and Coigach

Route 1: Ascent of Ben Mor Coigach from Acheninver youth hostel	37
Route 2: Ascent of Ben Mor Coigach from the Achiltibuie road	40
Route 3: Ascent of Cul Beag from Drumrunie	43
Route 4: Ascent of Cul Beag from Linneraineach	44
Route 5: Cul Beag to Stac Pollaidh link route	45
Route 6: Ascent to Stac Pollaidh's main col from Loch Lurgain	46
Route 7: Traverse of Stac Pollaidh's summit ridge	48
Route 8: Ascent of Cul Mor from Knockanrock	50
Route 9: Ascent of Cul Mor from the A835 via An Laogh	51
Route 10: Ascent of Cul Mor from Linneraineach via south-west face	52
Route 11: Cul Mor to Cul Beag link route	53
Route 12: Suilven approach from Elphin	55
Route 13: Suilven approach from Lochinver	56
Route 14: Suilven ascent from the north-east	57
Route 15: Suilven ascent from Inverkirkaig	57
Route 16: Suilven approach from Little Assynt	60
Route 17: Traverse of the Suilven summit ridge	61
Route 18: Canisp ascent from Little Assynt	62
Route 19: Canisp ascent from Loch Awe	62
Route 20: Canisp to Suilven link route	63

Route 21: Breabag ascent from Benmore Lodge..65
Route 22: Breabag ascent from Allt nan Uamh 66
Route 23: Breabag to Conival link route...67
Route 24: Ben More Assynt and Conival ascent from Inchnadamph................68
Route 25: The Oykell Horseshoe from Kinlochailsh 70
Route 26: Glas Bheinn and Beinn Uidhe ascent from Loch na Gainmhich.......73
Route 27: Beinn Uidhe to Conival/Ben Mor Assynt link route 76
Route 28: Ascent of Quinag from the east...79
Route 29: Ascents of Quinag from the north...81
Route 30: Ascent of Quinag from Tumore..82
Route 31: Quinag to Glas Bheinn link route..83
Route 32: Ascent of Meallan a Chuail and Beinn Leoid
  from Kinloch, Loch More...85
Route 33: Ascent of Beinn Leoid from Kylestrome via Glen Dubh....................86
Route 34: Ascent of Beinn Leoid and Meallan a Chuail from Loch na
  Gainmhich via Eas a Chuall Aluinn..87
Route 35: Beinn Leoid to Beinn Uidhe link route..90

The Far northwest and Reay Forest
Route 36: Ascent of Ben Stack from near Lochstack Lodge...............................93
Route 37: Ascent of Ben Hee from West Merkland..95
Route 38: Ascent of Meallan Liath from Achfary via Lone 98
Route 39: Ascent Meallan Liath from Aultanrynie 100
Route 40: Meallan Liath to Sabhal Beag link route...101
Route 41: Ascent of Meall Horn and The Sabhals from Achfary via Lone 102
Route 42: Direct ascent of Meall Horn from Lone...104
Route 43: Meall Horn/Creagan Meall Horn col to Arkle link route.................104
Route 44: Meall Horn/Creagan Meall Horn col to Foinaven link route...........105
Route 45: Ascent of Arkle from Achfary 106
Routes 46 and 47: Link routes from Arkle to Foinaven and Meall Horn..........108
Route 48: Ascent of Foinaven from the north-west...110
Route 49: Beinn Spionnaidh and Cranstackie from Carbreck 113
Route 50: Ascent of Ben Hope from Strath More..114

The East
Route 51: Ascent of Ben Loyal from Ribigill...117
Route 52: Ascent of Beinn Stumanadh from Loch Loyal 121
Route 53: Ascent of Ben Klibreck from Vagastie..124

Route 54: Ascent of Ben Klibreck from Altnaharra 125
Route 55: The full traverse of Kilbreck ridge from Crask Inn 126
Route 56: Ascent of Morven from Braemore 129

Longer Mountain Traverses
Route 57: The Assynt Horseshoe 131
Route 58: A Reay traverse 135
Route 59: A long ascent of Cranstackie 138

Interesting Low-Level Walks
Route 60: Eas a Chual Aluinn 141
Route 61: The Culnacraig coastal path 142
Route 62: To Sandwood Bay and Cape Wrath 143

Other Routes 145

Appendix A: Sources of information..146
Appendix B: The peaks (by height)...147
Appendix C: The peaks (alphabetically) 148
Appendix D: List of walking routes 149

The Mountains

1 Ben Mor Coigach
2 Cul Beag
3 Stack Polly
4 Cul Mor
5 Suilven
6 Canisp
7 Braebag
8 Ben More Assynt
9 Glas Bheinn
10 Quinag
11 Beinn Leoid
12 Ben Stack
13 Ben Hee
14 Meallan Laith Coire Mhic Dhughaill
15 Meall Horn
16 Arkle
17 Foinaven
18 Cranstackie
19 Ben Hope
20 Ben Loyal
21 Beinn Stumanadh
22 Ben Klibreck
23 Morven
24 Scaraben

Areas covered by the guide

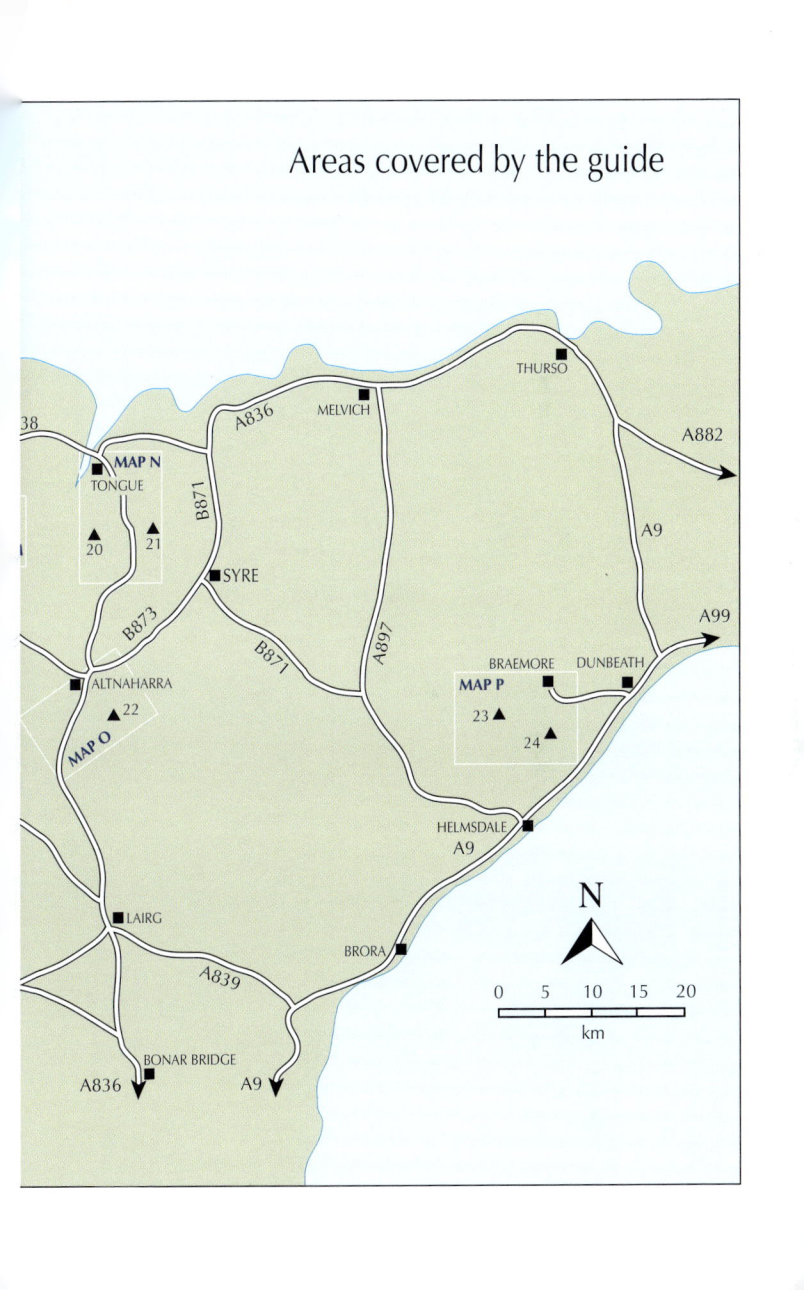

Map Key

— ridge

— river/watercourse

••• walking route

▪▪▪ village/habitation

≋ road

P parking

🌲 forest

▲ summit

✦ monument

⬭ coastal/inland waters

⋯ path/track

PREFACE

This book has been over four years in the making. When I first began the project I already had some knowledge of the far north of Scotland, having first visited at the age of 14 and a few times since then. However, as I began my further explorations I realised that the more I discovered, the more I found which still remained to be discovered!

Like any regular visitor to the Scottish highlands, I've had a truly mixed bag of weather to contend with, from snow down to sea level at Scourie in March, to a superb week of blazing sun in May when the beach at Oldshoremore put anything in Cornwall to shame!

In between there have been magical days of mixed sun and cloud (so atmospheric), along with those particularly Scottish specialities – mist and seemingly endless sluicing rain.

In truth it is precisely this variation which gives Scotland its special appeal, and I can honestly say that I have enjoyed every trip I've made to the area.

I hope that users of the book with get as much pleasure from exploring this excellent area as I have.

Andy Walmsley

The Lobster's Claw (Stack Polly), Route 7

INTRODUCTION

The 'far north' is one of Scotland's best-kept secrets. Despite its many attractions, the area is largely ignored by British holidaymakers, though it is popular with visitors from elsewhere in Europe. Even at the height of the summer season, the area is never really busy, and this is one of its attractions to the connoisseur who appreciates the solitude, the rugged coastline and the unique landscape with its bumpy gneiss moorland and jutting peaks.

The country's northern peninsula, with the remote headland of Cape Wrath at its tip, is covered in this guide as far as Ullapool in the south and Dunbeath in the east. The guide is selective rather than comprehensive, however, and readers will notice a bias towards the west side of the northern peninsula. This is intentional, as most of the rugged (and thus the most interesting) terrain is concentrated there; but Morven (the highest summit in the old county of Caithness) and its neighbour Scaraben, are included, along with a couple of other interesting routes on the eastern side. The far north-eastern corner of Caithness (the 'lowlands beyond the highlands'), including John o'Groats, Wick and Thurso, is not covered.

The area has some of the most challenging and spectacular

Sunset over Scourie Bay

mountains in the British Isles, including splendid peaks such as Suilven and Quinag, yet because they are mostly below Munro status most of the hills have been spared the worst excesses of exploitation. Nevertheless, the far north hills stand head and shoulders above many a Munro in terms of interest and character.

A large part of the area covered by the guide is made up of lumpy gneiss moorland, sprinkled with a multitude of tiny lochans, which form an unusual landscape. Readers who like wild, remote country with extensive vistas opening up around each corner will find many routes to their liking. There is a real feeling of spaciousness up here, which is often lacking further south.

Another jewel of the far north is the coastline. From Ullapool north to Cape Wrath, and then east as far as Strathy Point, the Atlantic seaboard threads a ragged line, encompassing wonderful little crofting settlements, spectacular headlands, excellent beaches, fjord-like sea lochs, fascinating offshore islands (including the Summer Isles and Handa Island), the British mainland's highest sea cliffs and two of Scotland's most celebrated sea-stacks – the Old Man of Stoer and Am Buachaille.

As if this were not enough, the area has limestone caves, Britain's highest waterfall and a number of interesting antiquities! Surely such variety in so small an area is unique.

Surprisingly, although this is the

Looking across to the mainland peaks from the Summer Isles

View north across Balnakeil Bay

farthest-flung corner of the British mainland, the mountains are all relatively accessible, being fairly close to roads in most cases. However, they are also quite well scattered, and for this reason it is difficult to climb a large number of them from one fixed base. The dedicated peak-bagger would have to move around by car quite a bit to collect them all, using a number of different bases. With this in mind, I have mentioned the best bases for each area at the end of the area introduction.

TOPOGRAPHY

Much of the southern area of the guide, Coigach and Assynt, consists of the characteristically choppy moor, composed of ancient gneiss rocks and made up of innumerable abrupt little hillocks cradling a multitude of tiny lochans. This terrain seldom rises much above 200m, leaving peaks such as Suilven standing in spectacular isolation. Many of the peaks consist of huge outcrops of Torridon sandstone, a rock which weathers into fantastic pinnacles and spires and which has a superb rough texture, ideal for scrambling.

Further north, above Rhiconich, there is more schist, giving a smoother more boggy type of moor, and rising from this are the majestic quartzite peaks of Arkle and Foinaven, characterised by their swooping ridges and dazzling screes.

Moving eastwards from the coast the mountains generally become less shapely and thus less interesting, but hills such as Ben Leoid, Ben Hee and the Munro Ben Klibreck give good walking in superb lonely terrain.

Even further east, the mountainous terrain of the west gives way to a bleak rolling moorland with very few interesting summits. The exception to this is the area immediately inland of Berriedale on the east coast, where outcroppings of sandstone have produced the distinctive peaks of Morven, Smean, Maiden Pap and Scaraben – well worth a visit.

Overlooking the north coast village of Tongue are the prominent isolated peaks of Ben Loyal (often given the sobriquet of 'Queen of Scottish Mountains') and Ben Hope (most northerly of the Munros). Ben Loyal is a shapely peak, but lacks the pinnacled ridges of Suilven or Stack Pollaidh, while Ben Hope is of simple form but is challengingly craggy, particularly its northern ridge, which provides the most difficult ascent route.

The coastline, especially in the west and north, is almost as spectacular as the mountains and boasts a number of features which are worth a visit. North from Ullapool, the coast skirts around Loch Kanaird and Ardmair Bay, then passes beneath the cliffs of Ben More Coigach, with the Summer Isles offshore at this point, before reaching the exposed headland of Rubha Coigeach. Turning abruptly southwest, the coast passes the extensive sands of Achnahaird Bay, and twists and turns around the innumerable

Loch Lurgainn from Stack Polly, Route 7

Loch Stack

inlets of Enard Bay (including Loch Inver) before encompassing a string of sandy beaches on the run out to the Point of Stoer, with its spectacular sea stack the Old Man of Stoer.

From here the shoreline penetrates deep inland, to the heads of the fjord-like lochs Glencoul and Glendhu, then threads a ragged line north, encompassing the island-studded Eddrachillis Bay. After sneaking past the Isle of Handa, the coast forms two more fjord-like sea lochs in Lochs Laxford and Inchard, before reaching the beach at Sandwood Bay.

Sandwood Bay would be a crowded and commercialised place if it were situated further south, or even if accessible by road, but it has escaped the attentions of the day-tripping crowds because of its remoteness. Its 2km of reddish sand, overlooked by the sea stack known as Am Buachaille, is completely unspoilt and often deserted.

North of the bay the coast becomes rugged again as it rises to the headland of Cape Wrath, with its stubby lighthouse. This is Britain's most remote headland (but not the most northerly). Turning east, the coast presents a series of high cliffs to the crashing seas of the Atlantic, the ones at Cleit Dubh being the highest on the British mainland, but these gradually subside into the gentle shores of the shallow Kyle of Durness with its mud flats and sand dunes.

Beyond the sandy headland of Fair Aird (variously referred to as Faraid Head or 'Far Out Head') a series of delectable coves with sandy beaches lead along to the mouth of Loch Eriboll, by far the largest of the 'fjords' along this coast. Eriboll is often used as a deep-water refuge by shipping during stormy weather.

The Kyle of Tongue, which is the next inlet along the coast, is completely different from the brooding Eriboll, being a shallow firth like the Kyle of Durness, but it is overlooked by the majestic Ben Loyal, giving it a scenic quality which is lacking in its neighbouring sea lochs.

Continuing east, the coast shortly reaches Bettyhill at the outlet of Strath Naver, which is the border of this area of the guide.

CLIMATE

Contrary to popular belief, the climate does not get worse the further north you go! In fact, the far north has a much more favourable climate than the central highlands. For example, average July rainfall in Fort William is over 5 inches, compared to about 3 inches at Inverness or Stornoway, and only 2.6 inches at Wick.

Like most of Scotland, May and June are the driest and sunniest months, but September/October can also give good sunny days, along with the low-angled sun which is so atmospheric. July and August provide the warmest weather, but rainfall averages are higher than in May or June and there is, of course, the midge problem to contend with at that time of year. If camping, it is worth remembering that exposed coastal sites suffer less from midges than more sheltered locations because of the sea breezes.

Another interesting fact about this area is that bad weather is often

Inverpolly

very localised. When rain and mist shroud the hills, a trip out onto one of the west coast headlands – such as Rubha Stoer or Rubha Coigeach – can often find brighter skies and no rain, although this fact is no consolation if your aim is to ascend the inland peaks!

Winter climbing is not much practised in the area covered by the guide because of the rarity of good conditions. Snowfall is not uncommon during winter, but rarely stays for long on the coastal hills. Inland peaks such as Ben Hee and Ben Klibreck generally hold more snow, but the winter climbing conditions found in the Cairngorms, for example, are not common in the guidebook area.

Access problems due to snow are rare, unless you intend to attempt to reach some remote location in a particularly bad winter, but notes on the accessibility of the roads in a severe winter are given below in 'Roads within the Area'.

PLANTS, BIRDS AND ANIMALS

Plant life in the far north is much the same as you might find in areas further south, such as the moorland of northern England. Some of the hills have a thick covering of heather, particularly on their lower slopes, and elsewhere there is rough moorland grass and sedge – often waterlogged – on a base of peat. Due to the scarcity of paths on the less popular hills, this can make for arduous approaches.

Apart from a few isolated exceptions, there is little forest in the guide area. The most extensive tree-covered area is the Dalchork Forest, north of Lairg, which is a remote man-made plantation of conifers. There are remnants of the natural forests which once covered this land, most notably around sea inlets near Lochinver, Inverkirkaig and Loch Nedd.

Birds are quite plentiful in the summer months – grouse are an obvious example, along with other moorland natives such as curlew and skylark. The characteristic songs of these birds are very atmospheric on a warm spring day in the hills. Birds of prey such as hen harriers, kestrels and owls may be seen, but are less common here than further south.

Along the coast, sea-birds such as guillemot, kittiwake, razorbill, fulmar and puffin, along with various gulls and gannets, abound. There is a bird sanctuary on Handa Island (ferry from Scourie or Tarbet), which is a must for anyone with an interest in ornithology.

Seals are another sight to look out for in coastal areas. Both common seals and the much larger grey seal are quite numerous around the north-west coast, and colonies of them can be seen in sea lochs such as Glencoul and Glendhu, either in the water or basking on the shore.

You may spot other wildlife such as fox, hare, red squirrel, badger, wildcat, otter and various species of vole and shrew. The north-west highlands is the last stronghold of many species which have all but disappeared from the areas further south. Deer are of course plentiful, and their numbers are controlled by an annual cull. Access to many of the far north hills is curtailed if there is 'stalking' going on, and it is always a good idea to check before setting out.

BASES

There is no shortage of accommodation available in the far north. The area boasts a multitude of hotels, B&Bs, campsites and self-catering cottages, chalets and hostels. In fact, there is such a wealth of choice that a comprehensive list would fill this book and probably a couple of others too! It is possible to obtain hotel or self-catering accommodation at any time of year, but most campsites are are only open from Easter to the end of September. Check before travelling. The best sources of information are the tourist offices/visitor centres listed in Appendix A.

Below is a summary of the main walking centres and the facilities to be found there. The list is not comprehensive, but short lists of convenient bases are given in the introductions to each area in the walks section of the guide.

Ullapool

This is the largest community in the area. A major fishing and ferry port, the town boasts a number of restaurants, hotels, guest houses and self-catering accommodation, as well as a campsite and youth hostel. Other amenities include a bank with cashpoint, supermarkets, a filling station, an excellent hardware store selling most camping utilities, and even a fish and chip shop!

Ullapool (photo: Andy Walmsley)

Boat trips to the Summer Isles during summer, and a car ferry to Stornoway in the Western Isles, are available.

Four miles (6.6km) north is the excellent campsite at Ardmair, on the shores of Loch Kanaird. This is a clean and well-equipped site with showers, laundry room, shop and restaurant. Chalets are also available for hire. The site has a very short season however: Easter to September at best.

Ullapool makes a good base for the Coigach peaks.

Bonar Bridge

This is a small village at the head of the Dornoch Firth. The iron bridge here replaced Telford's original, which used to carry the main A9 northwards before the building of the new bridge linking Tain and Dornoch.

The village has shops selling provisions, calor gas, films, etc, and a filling station, but no bank. Accommodation is available nearby at Ardgay, or further north at Lairg.

Access to Ledmore junction and thus to the Assynt hills, via Strath Oykell, or to Laxford bridge and the Reay Forest, via Loch Shin, is surprisingly easy from here. Ben Klibreck is also easily reached.

Lairg

This is a slightly larger village than Bonar Bridge with similar facilities. There are chalets for hire in the vicinity, notably at Rogart in Strath Fleet to the east.

Although Lairg, like Bonar Bridge, is on the eastern side of the northern peninsula, it lies close to the main through-routes, and post buses run regularly to various points north and west. It is thus more convenient than you might think as a base for visiting Assynt, Coigach and the Reay Forest, and has the advantage that accommodation on this side is generally cheaper than on the west coast.

Achiltibuie

This is one of the far north's special places. The 'village' is little more than a straggling group of houses strung out along the coast at the foot of Ben Mor Coigach and overlooking the Summer Isles, but it has a unique atmosphere: remote – some might say bleak – yet welcoming.

There is a hotel and self-catering cottages in the area, as well as a youth hostel at Acheninver (20 beds) a little to the south (GR043056), and a campsite by the rather exposed beach at Achnahaird (GR015136). Boat trips are available to the Summer Isles (but, appropriately enough, only in summer) – contact Iain McLeod at the post office.

Achiltibuie is located right at the foot of Ben Mor Coigach, and makes a good base for any of the Coigach mountains.

Inverkirkaig

This is a small, scattered, coastal settlement at the head of the tiny Loch Kirkaig. There are self-catering chalets

Achmelvich Bay and campsite at Lochinver (photo: Andy Walmsley)

and cottages here and a public telephone box, but not much else. The situation, looking out towards the Western Isles, is superb.

The well-known Achins bookshop and café are situated slightly inland at the start of the path to the Falls of Kirkaig.

Lochinver

A main centre on the north-west coast, Lochinver has all the necessary conveniences of civilisation, such as a bank with cash-point, filling station and two well-stocked grocery stores, as well as hotels, outdoor shop, the Assynt Visitor Centre and a wealth of self-catering accommodation. Baddidaroch, along the north side of Loch Inver, also has a good number of self-catering cottages for hire.

The nearest campsite is at Achmelvich, 3 miles (5km) north by Loch Roe. This is a good, reasonably priced, fairly well-equipped site (open March to September) close to the excellent sandy beach of Achmelvich Bay. There is also a youth hostel (38 beds – open March to September) here.

Stoer

Situated on the picturesque coast road between Lochinver and Kylesku, Stoer is merely a tiny crofting community with a small sandy beach (pleasant in good weather, but usually just bleak) and a post office with limited opening hours. Nearby is the rather basic campsite at Clachtoll (which has an attractive sandy cove). The scenery at Stoer is defaced by ramshackle mobile homes, which are common in the area.

Drumbeg

A slightly larger community than Stoer and rather more attractive, Drumbeg is situated further north along the same road. Its location is elevated, overlooking the rocky shore of Eddrachillis Bay and Oldany Island. There is a parking area with toilets, and a view indicator looking out across the bay with its multiple islands – a picturesque scene in good weather. There is also an hotel and a post office here.

Kylesku

Once an important staging post on the route north, the village of Kylesku is now much quieter. A new bridge (an elegant one, it must be said) means that the village is now bypassed by the A894, which sweeps effortlessly over the narrow Caolas Cumhang and Garbh Eilean to reach the Duartmore Forest. The name Caolas Cumhang means 'the narrow straight', and it is from a corruption of this name that the anglicised form, Kylesku, is derived.

Kylesku has its own inn, and boat trips are run from the village up the fjord-like Loch Glencoul to visit the Eas a Chual Aluinn waterfall – Britain's highest at 658ft.

There is also a good choice of accommodation in the vicinity, and this area makes a good base for both the Assynt peaks and also those of the Reay Forest, further north.

Brora

An east coast village, somewhat larger than those above, Brora has most amenities, including campsites, hotels, etc. Its location is rather inconvenient for the main mountains of the far north, but it does have the advantage of being served by the railway.

Helmsdale

Like Brora, Helmsdale is located on the east coast, is serviced by rail, and has a youth hostel and a tourist information office, as well as shops, hotels, etc. It is reasonably convenient for the eastern peaks such as Morven, and could also serve as a base for peaks such as Ben Klibreck if motorised transport is available.

About halfway between Brora and Helmsdale is a campsite (Crakaig Camping – GR960097). The site is basic and low priced, and is in an attractive setting by the beach at Lothbeg Point.

Scourie

This is a pleasant crofting village built in a natural bowl among low rocky hills and overlooking the sheltered Scourie Bay. There is a friendly hotel, expensive filling station, well-stocked provisions store/post office, and a number of self-catering cottages nearby. Scourie also has the best campsite in the far north. Reasonably priced, the site is clean and well laid out with terraced pitches overlooking the sea, and has a relaxed atmosphere. Free hot showers are available, along with a laundry room, a restaurant, and an affable owner who will allow dogs, provided they are exercised off the site (open from Easter to end of September – occasionally at other times if there is demand).

A boat runs (weather permitting) from the pier to the Handa Island Bird Sanctuary.

Scourie is a convenient base for the Reay Forest and the far north-west.

Rhiconich

Little more than a hotel with a few surrounding crofts and cottages, Rhiconich is the last outpost on the road to the north coast, and marks the junction with the branch road out to Kinlochbervie and Shiegra.

The hotel would make a good base for ascents of Arkle or Foinaven.

Dunbeath

This is a small, scattered village, located on the east coast in the far north-eastern corner of the guide area. Dunbeath has a camp site and a hotel, and is a convenient base for the exploration of the Morven group of hills.

Kinlochbervie

This is a major fishing port on the north-west coast, comparable to Ullapool in importance. Kinlochbervie is situated on a narrow neck of land between two sheltered bays – an ideal location for a port. It has a lonelier atmosphere than Ullapool, but does offer a range of accommodation and is conveniently situated in relation to the great peaks of Foinaven and Arkle.

Nearby is a lovely beach at Oldshoremore (campsites here and at Balshrick) and the start of the path to Sandwood Bay, one of the jewels of the coast.

Durness

Bleakly exposed atop rugged sea cliffs, Durness is at the northernmost point of the A838 road. The village itself consists only of a few scattered houses and a couple of shops, but in the vicinity are a number of attractions including a good campsite, a youth hostel, some spectacular beaches, the celebrated Cave of Smoo (with hotel) and the Balnakeil Craft Village. The latter is housed in converted old army buildings, which are numerous hereabouts.

Tongue

Tongue is an unremarkable village, clustered around a sharp road bend near the junction of the A838 and A836. It has two hotels, a youth hostel (on the shore of the Kyle of Tongue), a very small campsite and a post office.

The Kyle of Tongue Crossing (more of a causeway than a bridge) has bypassed the former road, which took a circuitous route around the southern shore of the Kyle. However, the old road is still worth driving for its superb views of Ben Loyal.

Tongue makes a convenient base for Ben Loyal, Ben Hope, Ben Stumanadh and Ben Klibreck.

GETTING THERE

Although situated in the farthest corner of the British mainland, the far north is not as difficult to reach as might be imagined. Excellent road links make Ullapool (for example) as accessible as many popular Scottish locations further south. For the southern Sassenach, the journey to Skye or Torridon can take just as long as that to the far north.

The A9, although not the most scenic of Scottish roads, makes for easy travel to Inverness, and links to Lairg, Helmsdale or Ullapool from there are excellent. For those who cannot face the drive, there are internal flights available to Inverness and Wick, or you could even let the train take the strain – the line meanders all the way up to Wick via Lairg, Helmsdale and Forsinard.

Once you are much north of Inverness, Royal Mail post buses provide the main system of public transport. These run regularly between all post offices in the far north, and a timetable is available from the Royal Mail on request. Note that, despite the name, you should not expect these post buses to actually be 'buses'. You are just as likely to find yourself travelling in a small van or estate car as in a purpose-built bus.

Summer Isles ferry

Roads within the Area

With the notable exception of the Parph and Cape Wrath, road access within in the area is very good, but not **too** good. You are never far from a road in this area, and all the peaks are fairly easily accessible, but there are a number of places where it is possible to get away from the car-borne tourist and feel the 'wilderness experience'. The inner reaches of Glen Dubh and Glen Coul (east of Kylesku), and the middle of the Inverpolly Forest (west of Cul Mor), spring immediately to mind.

Although the road network is quite comprehensive, many of the roads are single track, and outside the months of June, July and August they see little traffic. In early spring or in autumn it is possible to drive for miles along these roads without seeing a single vehicle. This is quite a contrast to areas south of Inverness, and it is one of the great charms of the far north.

If a winter trip is planned, it is worth remembering that road closures due to snow can occur in these parts, and in particularly bad weather it may be impossible to access anything beyond the main trunk routes.

Access to individual peaks is covered in the relevant route description in the walks section of the guide, but below is a brief description of each of the main access routes.

The view south from Achiltibuie

ROADS WITHIN THE AREA

A835 from Ullapool to Ledmore
17 miles (27km)
Winter access: usually kept open
An excellent two-lane trunk road giving good views of the Coigach peaks (especially the jutting prow of Sgurr an Fhidhleir). Long straights and easy bends mean fast progress. Knockanrock viewpoint and information centre at GR188090.

From Drumrunie (GR165054) to Achiltibuie
– with branches to Reiff and Achnahaird
15 miles (24km) excluding branches
Winter access: doubtful under snow
Unclassified single-track road, but easy. Passes the bases of Cul Beag and Stac Pollaidh (also passing the turning to Lochinver – see below), then descends to a junction at the south end of Achnahaird Bay. Right leads to the Achnahaird campsite and Rubha Mor (Rubha Coigeach); left leads south to Achiltibuie. A short branch road leads norh-west to Reiff, also linking with the Achnahaird road.

From Badnagyle (GR063113) to Lochinver
– 'The Mad Little Road of Sutherland', 11 miles (18km)
Winter access: best avoided in winter conditions
Unclassified single-track road. Starts easily, but becomes extremely tortuous. Gives spectacular glimpses of the Inverpolly peaks and Suilven as it traverses the lumpy moor west of Loch Sionascaig.

After wriggling around an inlet of Enard Bay, the road cuts across Rubha na Breige to the River Kirkaig (start of path to Falls of Kirkaig and Suilven, café and bookstore) and shortly enters Inverkirkaig (self-catering accommodation, telephone). A further climb takes the road over to Lochinver.

A837 from Invershin (GR574966) to Ledmore
26 miles (42km)
Winter access: rarely closed
Single-track trunk road. This is the main access from the east to Assynt and Coigach, so is usually kept open even in snowy weather. There are a few very short two-lane stretches, but these are best regarded as extended passing places. The road begins in rural semi-wooded terrain, then climbs gradually into open moorland. Good view of Suilven ahead as Ledmore is approached.

A837 from Ledmore (GR248124) to Lochinver
19 miles (30km)
Winter access: kept open in all but the most severe blizzards
Two-lane trunk road. After joining with the A835 at the Ledmore junction, the A837 becomes an excellent two-lane road. The road crosses the Kirkaig/Inver watershed then descends to Inchnadamph (private lodge and hotel with petrol pump, expensive). After passing the turning to Kylesku at Skiag Bridge, the road skirts along the shore of Loch Assynt to Lochinver.

B869 Assynt Coast Road, GR099235
(near Lochinver) to GR232314 (near Kylesku)
21 miles (34km)
Winter access: impassable under snow
This unclassified single-track road is considerably 'madder' than the 'Mad Little Road of Sutherland' (see above), with numerous climbs, descents and blind brows. The first section is enclosed and wooded, passing the branch to Achmelvich (youth hostel and campsite) before climbing into open country (excellent viewpoint on the left at GR078254). After passing the bleak campsite and small sandy beaches of Clachtoll and Stoer, the road swings inland to cross the neck of the Stoer headland to Clashnessie (branch road on the left leads to the Stoer lighthouse).

Beyond Clashnessie (sandy bay, ugly static caravans) the road crosses more moorland to reach Drumbeg (parking, toilets, hotel) in an elevated position overlooking Oldany Island, then descends to Nedd by the shore of the charming Loch Nedd, heavily screened by trees.

From here to the main road near Kylesku is the most demanding section. The road heads east to the A894 via an arduous series of ups and downs (the descent into, and climb out of, Gleann Ardbhair being particularly untamed), with glimpses of Quinag's impressive northern buttresses on the right.

A894 from Skiag Bridge to Laxford Bridge
23 miles (37km)
Winter access: usually kept open
Two-lane trunk road. The initial section, over the pass between Quinag and Glasven, has some tight and bumpy bends, but after Kylesku Bridge the road smoothes out and makes easy progress to Scourie (campsite, restaurant, hotel, post office, toilets). Continuing easily, the road passes a turning on the left to Foindle, Fanagmore and Tarbet (Handa Island ferry) before arriving at Laxford Bridge (no facilities).

Arkle and Loch Stack

A838 from Colabol junction (GR573099) to Laxford Bridge
34 miles (55km)
Winter access: usually kept open
Single-track A-road. Just north of Lairg on the road heading for Altnaharra and Tongue (A836), a left turn near the small group of buildings called Colaboll takes you onto the A838 to Laxford Bridge.

The A838 actually continues beyond Laxford Bridge to Tongue (description below), but a traveller between Lairg and Tongue would use the more direct A836.

Although single track, this road is open and quite straight, giving easy passage. The 17-mile (27km) shore of Loch Shin leads to a gentle ascent to the Loch More watershed, passing Loch Merkland and West Merkland (start of Ben Hee ascent) en route.

From the watershed (start of Beinn Leoid ascent) the road descends easily to skirt the southern shore of Loch More, with tremendous views of Ben Stack and Arkle ahead.

Beyond Achfary (routes to Arkle, Fionaven and the Sabhals), the road skirts along between Ben Stack and Loch Stack to eventually meet the two-lane A894 at Laxford Bridge.

Loch Eribol

A838 continuation, Laxford Bridge to Tongue
48 miles (77km)
Winter access: can be closed north of Rhiconich in severe weather

A mixture of two-lane and single-track A-road. Turning right at Laxford Bridge (the Scourie–Rhiconich road has priority) the A838 continues as a single-track road for about 300m then joins a smooth two-lane highway, like the A894, which then swoops its way to Rhiconich (hotel, petrol). A branch road (B801) runs out to Kinlochbervie from here, continuing as a single-track minor road as far as Sheigra, with a further branch to Oldshoremore. Sheigra is the closest approach by road to Cape Wrath, and the path to Sandwood Bay begins near here at Balshrick (campsite nearby).

North of Rhiconich, the A838 becomes single track and climbs up to Gualin House, with Foinaven towering to the right. Various small parking places along here provide starting points for Foinaven. Gualin House is now bypassed on its north-west side by a short new section of two-lane road, but single track takes over again as the road descends past Carbreck (start of Cranstackie ascent) to Kyle of Durness.

Just before Durness two-lane road reappears (at the junction with the short branch to the Cape Wrath Hotel and ferry) and this leads into the village itself. From Durness (hotels, 40-bed youth hostel, campsite, toilets, shop, tourist information) another short branch road leads out to the Balnakeil sand dunes, passing the interesting Balnakeil Craft Village en route.

The main road continues along the north coast (past Smoo Cave and various sandy beaches) before turning south to skirt Loch Eriboll (single track again).

After Eriboll, two-lane road climbs abruptly over a ridge to descend rapidly to a bridge at the head of Loch Hope (junction with minor road from Altnaharra). Another climb now leads up and over The Moine to the Kyle of Tongue.

The old road (single track) loops south around the head of the Kyle (still worth driving for its intimate views of Ben Loyal), but the new road spears straight across the shallow kyle on the Kyle of Tongue Crossing, which is more of a causeway than a bridge and leads quickly to the village of Tongue. The village has hotels, a basic campsite, shops, toilets and a 40-bed youth hostel (on the shore of the Kyle, next to the crossing).

A836 from Bonar Bridge to Bettyhill
59 miles (95km)
Winter access: likely to be closed in snowy weather
Remote, mainly single-track A-road. A fast stretch of two-lane road leads from Bonar Bridge to Lairg (all amenities), but the road then becomes single

Kyle of Tongue crossing and Ben Loyal

track and remains so all the way to Tongue, a distance of 36 miles (58km). However, the route is mainly over quite open terrain and progress is easy.

Undulating through plantations of conifers (Dalchork Forest), the road gradually gains height to pass the Crask Inn in open country just before the watershed. The road then descends into the shallow trough of Strath Vagastie (start of Ben Klibreck ascent) to eventually reach the scattered buildings at Altnaharra (hotel, post office) at the head of Loch Naver.

This is an important crossroads. The B873 heads east from here through Strath Naver, making a shorter route to Bettyhill (see below), while to the west a minor road goes via Alltnacaillich, at the foot of Ben Hope, to emerge on the A838 at Hope Lodge.

The A836 continues north, with Ben Loyal in view ahead, to traverse the west shore of Loch Loyal (Beinn Stumanadh group overlooking the opposite shore). At the north end of the loch, the road climbs moderately over a minor watershed, then descends to Tongue with improving views to the west.

Just south of the village, a branch road on the L provides a short-cut to Tongue village centre and the west, but the main road continues north to meet the A838 just above the village. The Durness–Bettyhill route has priority at this junction, but the road number A836 continues, now two lane (with two short stretches of single track), to Bettyhill and the border of the guide area.

B873 from Altnaharra junction to A836 near Bettyhill (GR708575)
20 miles (32km)
Winter access: sheltered, so usually open
Single track B-road. Commences with a scenic traverse of Loch Naver's north shore (many picturesque parking places) before turning north into Strath Naver – a very colourful and pleasing valley. The road makes easy progress throughout, passing a junction with the B871 to Kinbrace at Syre (11 miles from Altnaharra), and reaches the A836 at Leckfurin, just south of Bettyhill.

It is worth mentioning that the River Naver carries quite a large volume of water and has only easy rapids. To the author's untrained eye it would appear to be a prime candidate for kayaking or river rafting. From Loch Naver to Invernaver (the mouth of the river) is a distance of some 16 miles (26km).

Minor road from Altnaharra to Hope Lodge via Alltnacaillich
20 miles (32km)
Winter access: often closed by snow
Single-track road. Whilst having no major difficulties, this road is narrow

and, in parts, rough. It is the most convenient access road for the ascent of Ben Hope. At Allnabad, 8½ miles or 14km from Altnaharra, is the junction with the unsurfaced Bealach nam Mierleach, or Robber's Pass, a possible mountain bike route, passing Gobernuisgach Lodge and emerging at West Merkland (start of Ben Hee ascent). A branch route from this goes via Glen Golly to Strath Dionard (by Foinaven) with a further branch path crossing the Arkle/Meall Horn col to reach the bothy at Lone, on the shore of Loch Stack. These last two routes are, however, not mountain-bike friendly, judging by the anti-cycling notices erected by the estate.

East Coast Road (A9) from Dornoch Bridge to Dunbeath
47 miles (75km)
Winter access: always kept open
A major two-lane trunk road, the A9 can be busy in summer, but usually makes for fast progress up the east coast. It should be said that this is the most scenic stretch of the A9, the section beyond Helmsdale having some steep climbs and descents with excellent sea views.

Am Buachaille and Sandwood Bay, Route 62

USING THE GUIDE

The walks in this book are grouped firstly under geographical area headings, and secondly under mountain massifs. The majority of walks described are ascents of peaks or mountain traverses, and as such they are quite exacting. They involve rough terrain, and the text of the guide assumes the reader has a reasonable level of physical fitness and some experience of mountainous country.

Sketch maps are provided throughout the guide, but these are intended only to provide an overview of the route. Anyone undertaking the routes should use Ordnance Survey Landranger maps in conjunction with the book (see 'Maps', below). Details are given at the start of each route of the relevant sketch map and Landranger map.

It is difficult to attempt to grade the routes and estimate a reasonable time allowance for their completion. Grading can be a very subjective thing. For example a super-fit hill-runner may regard the rough ascent of Arkle as an easy outing, while an unfit person would find even the walk to the Eas a Chual Aluinn waterfall 'strenuous'. Similarly, time allowances are affected by differences in an individual's level of fitness or approach (lightweight or comprehensively equipped), competence on the terrain, the weather and a multitude of other factors.

For this reason neither grades nor times are given for the routes, and instead figures are provided for distance (measured from OS Landranger maps) and overall height gain (calculated from the same maps). Any competent hill-walker should be able to estimate the time required based on these figures, the route description and their own individual factors. A note of caution, though – Scottish terrain often means that more time is required than for a route of similar distance/ascent in, for example, the English Lake District, and it is also worth remembering that the distances quoted are map-measured kilometres, which are often a little shorter than kilometres actually walked on the ground. If you are not experienced on Scottish routes, add an allowance – say 20% – onto your estimated time. All the figures provided for distance and height gain are for round trips (returning to starting point) unless otherwise stated.

MAPS

Ordnance Survey Landranger sheets 9, 10, 15, 16 and 17 amply cover most of the area of the guide, but sheet 19 is required for Ullapool and Ardmair. The John o'Groats corner of the far north is covered on sheets 11 and 12, but this is outside the area covered by this guide. Visitors to the far north should be equipped with these maps, and the route descriptions in the book are designed to be used in conjunction with the relevant OS maps.

ESSENTIAL EQUIPMENT

When travelling or hill-walking in the far north, the equipment requirements are much the same as for any other part of Britain.

Waterproof clothing is an obvious essential at any time of year – preferably made from a breathable material, as summer conditions can often consist of relatively warm but wet weather, which can be very sticky in a non-breathable cagoule.

For any serious walking on these hills, my recommendation would be for leather boots with gaiters, unless the weather and terrain are very dry (rare – especially the latter). Fabric boots with a waterproof membrane tend to be very hot and are not as durable as leather ones. If wearing lightweight fabric boots or if hill-running, expect to have wet feet for much of the time!

Another common enemy in the summer months (normally late May to early September) is the dreaded Scottish midge. If conditions are windless, warmish and damp (quite common) then the beasties will be out in force. They are less of a problem during the day, when you tend to be walking and the sun is high (midges don't like direct sun as a rule), but can be a major irritation in the evenings. If camping, preferably choose a tent with mosquito netting which is advertised as Scottish-midge-proof (i.e. ultra fine). The better quality British manufacturers tend to understand this quite well, but makers of cheaper tents sometimes overlook this aspect. Certain upmarket foreign manufacturers, who should know better, can also be found wanting in this respect. You have been warned.

As regards repellents, the time-honoured Jungle Formula is about as good as you are going to get, but midges will certainly find places you have missed when applying it, even if it is above the hairline or inside clothing! Lesser repellents, based on citrus oils, tend to smell more pleasant, but are generally quite ineffective against the Scottish beastie.

A more effective 'in-camp' or 'outside-pub' strategy against midges is to create an exclusion zone with some midge-unfriendly vapours or fumes. You have two choices for this task, midge candles or midge coils. Candles are susceptible to breezes (more so than midges, which is unfortunate), but do have the advantage of smelling reasonably pleasant. Coils are fairly breeze-proof and very effective, but have the disadvantage of giving off quite noxious smoke. It all depends whether you prefer smoke or midge bites.

Winter expeditions to the hills of the far north may demand full winter equipment, including ice-axes and crampons, but full winter conditions are not as common in these parts as in eastern ranges such as the Cairngorms, due to the warm west-coast influences. If tackling these hills in winter, full equipment should be carried as a precaution, but perfect Alpine conditions are the exception rather than the rule.

MOUNTAIN BIKES

Mountain bikes are not exactly welcomed with open arms by landowners in the far north. Although there are a number of likely looking routes through the hills, the local landowners seem mostly hostile towards what is now a booming activity.

Certain routes are quite tempting and rideable (eg. the Bealach nam Meirleach from West Merkland – GR384329 – to Strath More near Ben Hope), but many others are either forbidden or have the kind of boggy terrain which renders a bike a liability rather than an advantage.

Keen bikers will probably find enough routes to keep them entertained (many of the single-track roads are quiet and pleasant to cycle along), but should not expect a wonderland of well-graded wilderness tracks.

GAELIC AND NORSE PLACE-NAMES

The vast majority of place-names in this area are of Gaelic (pronounced 'gallic') origin, and many of them have escaped the anglicising which has afflicted much of the southern highlands. The logic of Gaelic spelling and pronunciation is something of a mystery to most Sassenachs (non-highlanders), and is a major obstacle to Sassenach guide-book writers. However, where guidance can be reliably given it is provided.

Some peak names have both an anglicised and a Gaelic version, and in some of these cases the original Gaelic is still the preferred version – for example Glas Bheinn is still used rather than Glasven – but in others the anglicised version has taken over – for example Quinag instead of Cuinneag. In general I have followed the Gaelic usage, although in the case of Stac Pollaidh the commonly used anglicised version appears in the text and on the maps. For peaks where both forms are in common use (whether on maps or in literature) there is reference to both versions.

The Norse influence is also quite prominent in some areas, and some place-names are a combination of both Gaelic and Norse – Suilven is a corruption of the Norse 'sul' (a pillar) and the Gaelic 'bheinn' (a mountain). The suffix 'val' on names such as Conival (also commonly seen on Hebridean islands) is a corruption of the Norse 'fjall' (a mountain), and this is much used in southern Scotland and northern England as 'fell'.

ASSYNT AND COIGACH

Assynt and Coigach together have such a rich array of mountains and spectacular coastal features that they are almost worth a guidebook all of their own. It would be quite possible to have a tremendous two-week holiday without ever going beyond this area. Peaks such as Cul Mor and Cul Beag, Beinn Mor Coigach, Quinag, Suilven and the giants of Conival and Ben More Assynt provide ample scope for the peak-bagger, while the coast has more than enough interest for the most avid beachcomber. The headlands of Rubha Coigach and Rubha Stoer have a number of interesting little coves and inlets, and the Old Man of Stoer is one of Scotland's most spectacular sea stacks.

Good bases for the exploration of Assynt and Coigach include Ullapool, Ardmair, Achiltibuie, Elphin, Inchnadamph, Lochinver, Inverkirkaig and Achmelvich/Stoer.

Ben Mor Coigach, 743m (2438ft)

This multi-peaked mountain is a prominent object from any point along the Ardmair–Drumrunie–Loch Lurgain roads. Its south-west ridge (Garbh Choireachan) forms an imposing wall overlooking Ardmair Bay and Isle Martin. As Drumrunie is approached, a magnificent jutting triangle of rock, like the prow of some immense ship, comes into view. This is the peak of Sgurr an Fhidhlier – the 'fiddler's peak' – the most spectacular feature of the massif, which overlooks and completely overshadows the subsidiary peak of Beinn an Eoin.

A complete round of all the tops of Beinn Mor Coigach makes a demanding but very rewarding outing.

Route 1: Ascent of Ben Mor Coigach from Acheninver youth hostel

Distance:	16km
Height gain:	914m
Map:	A
OS Map:	Landranger 15

WALKING IN SCOTLAND'S FAR NORTH

This is the shortest approach to the main summit of Ben Mor Coigach, but it is also the steepest and one of the roughest. It is also the least convenient to approach by car, unless it is combined with a visit to Achilitibuie or a stay at the Acheninver youth hostel.

Leave Acheninver and walk along the road to Culnacraig, continuing onto the coastal path (south of the buildings). Follow the path for a short distance only before leaving it to strike directly up the imposing face of Garbh Choireachan. This is a steep and unrelenting climb, which becomes rougher and more scree-covered as height is gained. The consolation is the terrific view,

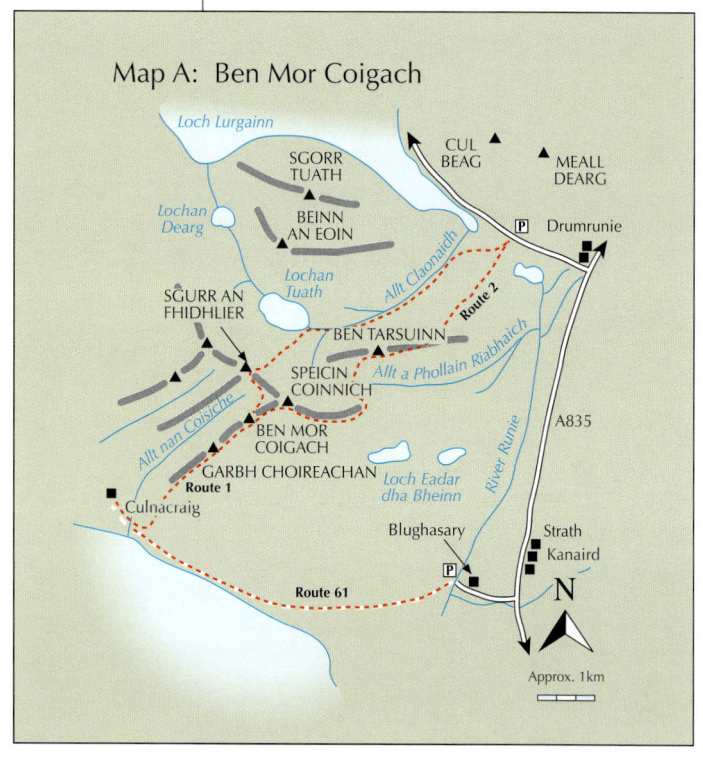

Map A: Ben Mor Coigach

Route 1: Ascent of Ben Mor Coigach from Acheninver

which opens up behind as you climb. The Summer Isles are especially well seen from here, and the chain of the Western Isles can be viewed on a clear day. The scale of the scene is more apparent if the Stornoway car ferry happens to be crossing the bay from Ullapool – its size completely dwarfed by the vast sea-scape of The Minch.

The steepness of the climb eventually eases, laying back onto the summit ridge of Garbh Choireachan, which is pleasingly narrow. The ridge leads easily along to a point where it broadens into a grassy plateau with sandy outcrops. The summit of the mountain is at the northern edge of this plateau. The simplest return is by your outward route.

Carn Conmheall from Culnacraig

> **Alternative**: If a longer return is required, it is quite possible to continue to Sgurr an Fhidhlier (see Route 2 for more details) then descend westward to traverse the subsidiary ridge of Beinn nan Caorach to its terminus at Carn Conmheall. A descent of the easy slopes to the south or west will then return you to the coast road between Culnacraig and Acheninver.

Route 2: Ascent of Ben Mor Coigach from the Achiltibuie road

Distance:	15km
Height gain:	914m
Map:	A
OS Map:	Landranger 15

About 2km (1¼ miles) from the Drumrunie junction along the road to Achiltibuie, there is good parking on both sides of the road, near spot height 113m on the OS Landranger map (GR149060). From here it is possible to make a beeline between lochans across marshy ground to an obvious gully, which carries Lochanan Dubha's main feeder stream through the broken crags of Beinn Tarsuinn.

Ascent of this gully is easy, especially on the left, and leads you onto the broad sandstone plates of Beinn Tarsuinn's east ridge (traces of a path). Easy walking over subsidiary tops soon brings the summit cairn into view, and the first route choice now presents itself.

The standard route to Ben Mor Coigach's summit ridge heads up a steep and featureless grass slope to the col west of Speicin Coinnich, but it is far more interesting to veer south across a shallow corrie and get onto the foot of the east ridge of the mountain, which affords an excellent rocky staircase to Speicin Coinnich's narrow summit arête. The view from here is superb, with Loch Kanaird, Isle Martin and Ardmair Point well displayed, and a good perspective on Stac Pollaidh and Cul Beag across Ben Tarsuinn and Beinn Eun.

Descending westward to the col, the 'normal route' is joined, and a good path climbs easily onto the sandy top of the mountain's main ridge, which leads all the way to the final top of Garbh Choireachan, overlooking Culnacraig and Loch Broom (see Route 1).

The main summit lies slightly north of the main ridge line and is reached across a wide grassy depression, but proves to be probably the least interesting of Ben Mor

Route 2: Ascent of Ben Mor Coigach from Achiltibuie road

Coigach's many tops, being merely a flat area with an inferior view. The much more exciting Sgurr an Fhidhleir beckons from the north, and a curving descent across easy slopes brings you to the head of a broad gully leading down to Lochan Tuath. This gully makes a good descent route, but Sgurr an Fhidhleir is much too good to miss out. An easy slope of sandy ground with broken sandstone outcrops leads to the summit cairn, which is perched on the very edge of a massive precipice falling to the western shore of the lochan.

The view is spectacular, especially into the profound gulf immediately north, with Beinn Eun at its far side and a bird's-eye view of Lochan Tuath with its sandy beach beckoning almost directly below. Those with surplus energy might like to tackle Beinn Eun, but if not, return to the col and descend the gully below it, which is steep but not difficult and leads to an increasingly distinct path heading down to the beaches of Lochan Tuath.

Beyond the lochan the path, now quite distinct, follows an old moraine ridge for a time, but loses itself among marshy ground after a while, eventually reappearing on the south bank of the Allt Claonaidh with the road almost in sight. Most of this descent is pretty wet underfoot, and it seems longer than it really is, but after an eternity of squelching the path drops more steeply with the stream now in a rocky little gorge on the left. This is the time to veer to the right towards the car-parking place. Any temptation to stay with the Allt Claonaidh should be resisted, as this leads to a morass of boggy grass at the head of Loch Lurgainn. An easterly line will take you across relatively pleasant ground to reach the road near to the car.

Alternative: A different approach to Speicin Coinnich is available from Blughasary, off the A835 at GR134014. From the footbridge here, a good vehicle track heads off northwards to climb easily into the corrie of Loch Eadar dha Bheinn (the 'loch between the hills'), from where it is a simple matter to climb onto the east ridge of Speicin Coinnich.

WALKING IN SCOTLAND'S FAR NORTH

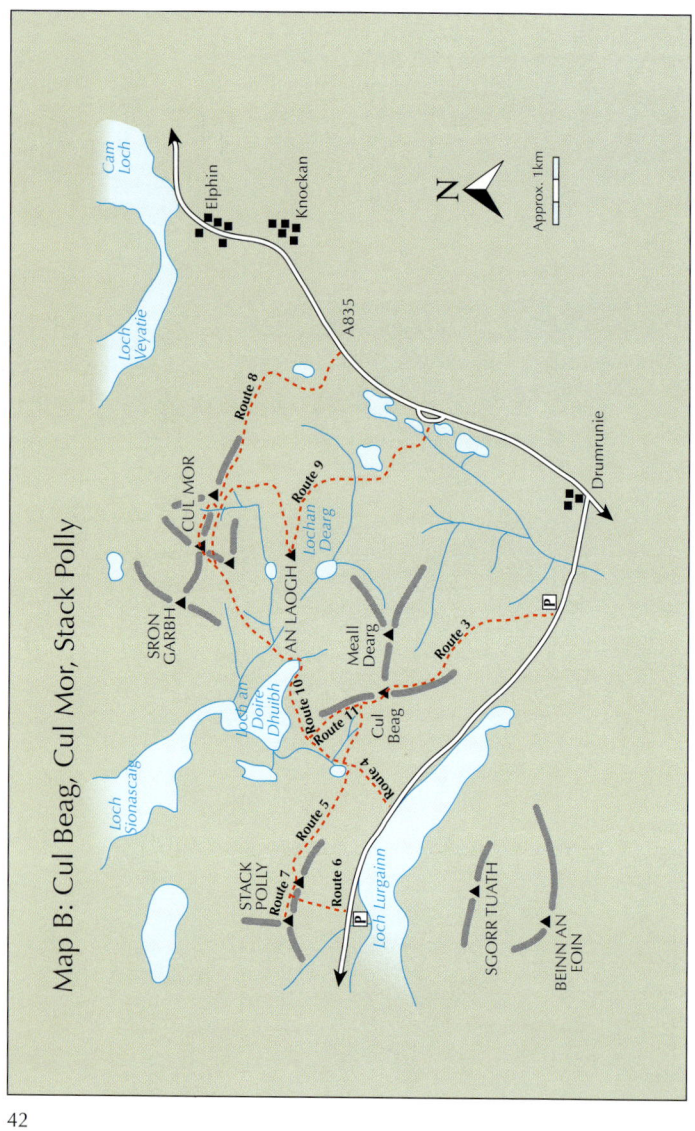

Map B: Cul Beag, Cul Mor, Stack Polly

Cul Beag, 769m (2523ft)

This imposing wedge of sandstone is a prominent object in many views of the Coigach area, but is often overlooked as the cameras aim for more photogenic subjects. It may not have the spiky profile of Stack Polly, the notched splendour of Suilven or the graceful sweeps of Cul Mor, but Cul Beag is a noble peak and well worth climbing for its own sake.

Two routes to the top are described below, and each has its own merits.

Route 3: Ascent of Cul Beag from Drumrunie

Distance:	3.1km
Height gain:	670m
Map:	B
OS Map:	Landranger 15

This route actually starts about 1.6km (1 mile) from the Drumrunie road junction at the point marked with spot height 113m on the OS Landranger map (GR149060). Near this point, there are a number of good parking places by the roadside.

The route is longer than that from Linneraineach (see Route 4), but affords a more scenic final approach to the summit along the top of the western cliffs.

From point 113m, head north through thick heather and bracken to reach the obvious top of Creag Dhubh, then follow the broad ridge up and over an unnamed top (c.460m) and across a wide saddle to reach the foot of Cul Beag's final summit wedge. Keep progressively further west as you climb the next section. The terrain becomes gradually more bare and rocky, and you will eventually emerge on the edge of the west face of the hill. The edge of the crags now provides an excellent guide to the top, with spectacular views down to the Achiltibuie road and Loch Lurgainn below.

Alternative: A longer and rougher route, which may appeal to those with the pioneering spirit (or just a desire to be different), starts from the A835 road near Knockanrock. An old loop of single-track road branches off the new road about 1km south of the Knockanrock visitor centre and leads to the start of a stalker's/fisherman's path at GR183081 (marked with spot height 245m on the Landranger map). The path skirts the southern edge of Lochan Fada and heads off into the heather to reach the larger Loch nan Ealachan. From here keep on in a westerly direction to gain the broad spur of Creag Dhuibh, which leads to the foot of Meall Dearg – Cul Beag's lower east summit. A stiff pull up over heather and sandstone rocks leads to the top of this eastern outlier, and the main summit is then only a short grassy climb away.

Route 4: Ascent of Cul Beag from Linneraineach

Distance:	6.5km
Height gain:	701m
Map:	B
OS Map:	Landranger 15

About 400m east of the cottage at Linneraineach, a small path leaves the road to climb obliquely up through a sparse group of trees towards the broad saddle (or moor) which separates Stack Polly from Cul Beag. This path is quite distinct and is identified by a notice board sprouting from the heather a few metres above the road. Parking is available at various points along the roadside near Linneraineach.

Start up this path, following it until it levels out by the shore of Lochan Fhionnlaidh. Turn off onto rough heather moor, aiming for the col between Cul Beag's main summit and its prominent northern outlier. A more direct line to this col is possible from the path's start, but this entails far more rough wet ground and isn't recommended.

A roughly westward beeline from the lochan, up progressively steeper ground, will bring you to the col, where conditions underfoot improve markedly. The final climb up the north ridge is steep, and in places loose, but gives no problems in reasonable conditions, and leads directly to the flat summit area.

ROUTE 5: CUL BEAG TO STAC POLLAIDH LINK ROUTE

Views from here are spectacular on a clear day, and it is well worth descending slightly along the edge of the western ramparts for the views down these spectacular crags.

The return to Linneraineach is best made by the outward route, unless it is intended to include other peaks in the outing.

Route 5: Cul Beag to Stac Pollaidh link route

Distance:	5km
Height gain:	442m summit to summit
Map:	B
OS Map:	Landranger 15

Loch Lurgainn and Cul Beag from Stack Polly

Stack Polly's attractions are best reserved for a sunny day, to be savoured in a leisurely fashion, but if a more demanding outing is desired it can be combined with the ascent of Cul Beag.

Assuming that you have one vehicle, parked near Linneraineach, then the best plan would be to tackle Cul Beag first by Route 4 (see above), returning to Lochan Fhionnlaidh, then to head west-north-west across rough and taxing moor to reach the path around the foot of Stack Polly's eastern buttress. A choice of routes is then available (see Stac Pollaidh section below).

After exploring the ridge, a quick descent can be made via the very eroded 'tourist route', and the road then followed back to the parking place near Linneraineach.

45

Stac Pollaidh (Stack Polly), 613m (2011ft)

Stack Polly ('the peak of the bog') is undoubtedly the most popular summit described in this book. The combination of easy access and a shapely profile are magnetic attractions for many visitors to Coigach. The peak stands in an isolated position overlooking Loch Lurgainn to the south and Loch Scionascaig to the north. It is well separated from its nearest neighbour, Cul Beag (see above), giving it a presence which belies its meagre altitude, but the jewel in Stack Polly's crown is its prickly summit ridge.

Route 6: Ascent to Stac Pollaidh's main col from Loch Lurgain

Distance:	3.2km
Height gain:	550m
Map:	B
OS Map:	Landranger 15

Stack Polly

ROUTE 6: ASCENT TO STAC POLLAIDH'S MAIN COL

Looking north across Inverpolly from Stack Polly

The usual routes to the summit ridge of Stack Polly aim to reach the obvious col near the eastern end of the ridge. The normal route is the direct path from the car park (GR108095) by the shore of Loch Lurgainn, which makes a beeline to the col. The path is free of difficulties, apart from steepness and erosion, and arrives dramatically on the crest of the ridge with a superb view of the Inverpolly Forest and Suilven.

Those with a desire to be different have three alternatives available. The first is a path which branches from the normal route on the flattish section just after the initial pull up from the car park (c.200m). This leads around the foot of the eastern buttress to climb to the main col from the north via a very eroded set of zig-zags.

The second alternative is the obvious gully to the left of the standard route, which is easily identified by its tongue of sandy coloured scree. The gully is steep and loose but without technical difficulties and reaches the ridge crest among sandstone pinnacles.

The more adventurous may prefer to consider a third alternative. Take the path around the eastern end of the peak as if heading for the eroded northern zig-zags, but leave the path at the foot of the East Buttress and make a direct scrambly ascent to the East Top. This route looks a little intimidating, but is in fact very easy (much harder scrambles await on the ridge) and is a much better approach than the over-used 'tourist paths'.

Route 7: Traverse of Stac Pollaidh's summit ridge

Distance:	variable
Height gain:	variable
Map:	B
OS Map:	Landranger 15

Now the fun begins! Assuming you have used the East Buttress route and are standing on the East Top (see Route 6) the first difficulty faces you immediately. The crossing of the cleft separating the East Top from the rest of the ridge involves a scramble up 5–6m (15–20ft) of steep rock. A couple of alternative lines exist, the easiest being further to the right (north). It is possible to avoid the difficulty altogether by descending a little from the cleft to follow a thin path along the northern flank to the main col. Now continue west and scramble up a steep step (easier lines to left and right) to reach the main spine of the ridge, which offers almost limitless route choice as the spiky sandstone pinnacles are traversed or avoided, depending on determination and courage! The northern slopes hereabouts are very broken, being mainly composed of easy gullies and scree slopes, so avoiding the crest is relatively easy.

Eventually the ridge narrows between gullies and is simultaneously barred by a little 'gendarme' – Stack Polly's 'mauvais pas'. This is the only route to the highest top, and forms a sort of drawbridge to the castle of the summit – a drawbridge which is permanently stuck in the half-open position.

The traverse of this little tower (no more than 2–2½m (7–8ft) high) is easy and has good holds, but it can feel quite exposed if the weather is windy. Wet rock would not pose a problem on this grippy sandstone, but ice

ROUTE 7: TRAVERSE OF STAC POLLAIDH'S SUMMIT RIDGE

would make the 'gendarme' decidedly dodgy. A bypass route via a loose and earthy gully does exist on the northern side, but this is much more unpleasant than crossing the tower.

Once over the 'mauvais pas' the main summit of the mountain is soon underfoot. The 'gendarme' has to be reversed to get down, but feels much easier in the opposite direction. If an alternative descent from the centre section of the ridge is desired, the northern slopes can be descended almost anywhere to join a traversing path on a shelf below. This leads back round the foot of the Eastern Buttress to rejoin the 'tourist' path just above the Loch Lurgainn car park.

On the summit ridge of Stack Polly (photo: Andy Walmsley)

Cul Mor, 849m (2785ft)

Cul Mor ('the big back') is a prominent object when travelling north along the A835. Not as shapely as Suilven, its lower neighbour, it is nevertheless an attractive hill and well worth climbing for its views alone. The panorama from the south top (Creag nan Calman) is particularly fine, with the noble peaks of Cul Beag and Stack Polly towering majestically over the wilds of the Inverpolly Forest.

Cul Mor is seen at its most impressive from the lower eastern slopes of either of these peaks, when the massive south-western wall of the mountain is fully appreciated (though not, perhaps, by those about to climb it).

Route 8: Ascent of Cul Mor from Knockanrock

Distance:	10km
Height gain:	732m
Map:	B
OS Map:	Landranger 15

There is ample parking by the main A835 road, almost opposite the Knockanrock information centre, and a good path starts from here and winds its way up into the hills, heading for the twin summits of Cul Mor.

Follow the path through the remains of an old deer fence and above the shore of Lochan Fhionnlaidh to emerge on the broad back of the Meallan Diomhain ridge, where there is a prominent cairn. The good gravelly surface now ends abruptly and the path becomes less distinct on peaty ground, though still easy to follow. As height is gained the terrain becomes more stony and the line is marked by a succession of tiny highland cairns, leading to the broad summit of Meallan Diomhain (pronounced 'mi-allan jee-vine').

A short descent is now necessary before you can get to grips with the final summit mass of the mountain, but take a few minutes to decide on your onward route. The easiest line crosses almost due west to the stream which emerges from Cul Mor's eastern coire over a series of rocky steps. This route has the gentlest gradients and is safer in mist, as the stream acts as a guide all the way to the headwall of the coire, immediately under the saddle between Cul Mor's two summits. Once on this sandy col, it is a simple matter of turning right for the main summit or left for Creag nan Calman.

The second option is to head further right (north-west) from the top of Meallan Diomhain, climbing a steep grass slope to reach the bouldery crest of the north-east ridge, then climbing this to the top. This option is harder than the first, but is more sporting and gives a more dramatic arrival at the summit.

The views are tremendous, looking out over Loch Veyatie to Suilven and Canisp to the north and over the Inverpolly Forest to the south and west, but for an even better view of Inverpolly, you need to cross to Creag nan Calman. This is a simple matter of descending to the main ridge col and climbing up an easy slope to the subsidiary summit. From here, tremendous crags fall to the shore of Loch an Doire Dhuibh, between Cul Mor and Cul Beag, and this view will give you a true appreciation of what is required in the crossing between the two peaks (Route 11).

Assuming you are not crossing to Cul Beag, descent is best made via the eastern coire route, which leads easily back to Meallan Diomhain, from where you can pick up the good path back to Knockanrock.

Route 9: Ascent of Cul Mor from the A835 via An Laogh

Distance:	13km
Height gain:	792m
Map:	B
OS Map:	Landranger 15

About 800–900m south of the Knockanrock parking, a loop of old road leaves the A835 (well marked on OS Landranger 15 with a spot height at 245m). Parking can be found here or at Knockanrock.

A good path leaves the old road loop to wind around to (and beyond) the shore of Loch nan Ealachan. Leave the path at the west side of the loch and head north, crossing the Allt an Loin Duibh and ascending the rough facing slope. A band of crag can be seen bounding the rising prow of An Laogh, and once above this turn north-west to climb above the crags to the 546m summit.

An Laogh could be bypassed altogether by contouring around its eastern slopes to the foot of Cul Mor (Creag nan Calman), but the view of Inverpolly and Loch Sionascaig from this modest top makes the extra effort well worthwhile.

From the summit, descend the top edge of the northern crags for 1km to reach the watershed between the minor stream systems of Lochan Dearg a Chiul Mhoir to the west and Loch an Laoigh to the east. From here climb directly north up a grassy spur to the right of a prominent ravine to a small unnamed lochan nestled under Meallan Diomhain. Easy slopes to the north-west now lead to the foot of Cul Mor's summit mass, where Route 8 is joined.

Route 10: Ascent of Cul Mor from Linneraineach via south-west face

Distance:	13km
Height gain:	975m
Map:	B
OS Map:	Landranger 15

Start as for Route 4 on Cul Beag, climbing easily up onto the moor by Lochan Fhionnlaidh, but continue along the main path, which descends through sparse birch woods (the Doire Dubh or 'dark woods') to the eastern end of Loch an Doire Duibh. Cul Mor looks truly formidable from here, but the climb is not as bad as it looks.

This south-west face of Cul Mor rises in two stages, with an easier-angled shelf in between. The first steep slope is grassy and leads, after a fair amount of plodding, onto the 'shelf', which gives easier progress for a couple of hundred feet. Aim in a more northerly direction, heading for a deep stream gully below a prominent spur falling from the summit of Creag nan Calman. This gully is steep and loose in places, but it leads without technical difficulty to the col between the two main tops of Cul Mor. Either the main summit or Creag nan Calman can then be visited easily.

Route 11: Cul Mor to Cul Beag link route

Distance:	4km
Height gain:	700m summit to summit
Map:	B
OS Map:	Landranger 15

This route takes in both Cul Mor and Cul Beag in the same outing, though this is a tough proposition for strong walkers only.

From the col on the main ridge of Cul Mor, descend northwards down the steep gully mentioned above (Route 10), initially broad but with a narrower section lower down (take care). This leads on to the lower plinth, or shelf, on which the mountain stands. Cross the plinth and make a final grassy descent through bands of crag to the valley floor. Cross the Allt an Loin Duibh and reach the eastern end of Loch an Doire Duibh.

Now skirt the shore of the loch on a good path among picturesque birch woods to a point where the path begins a gradual ascent south-west towards Lochan Fhionnlaidh en route for Linneraineach on the Drumrunie–Achilitibuie road. Leave the path here and climb directly up to Cul Mor's prominent northern outlier. This is a steep and relentless climb, but there is ample excuse to stop and admire the stupendous view in retrospect; you will surely marvel at your route of descent from Cul Mor, which looks particularly impressive from here. Once over the summit of the northern top, a loose eroded path leads up the final slope to the main summit of the mountain.

WALKING IN SCOTLAND'S FAR NORTH

Descent can be made via the ridge of Meall Dearg/Creag Dhubh to reach the A835 1km south of Knockanrock.

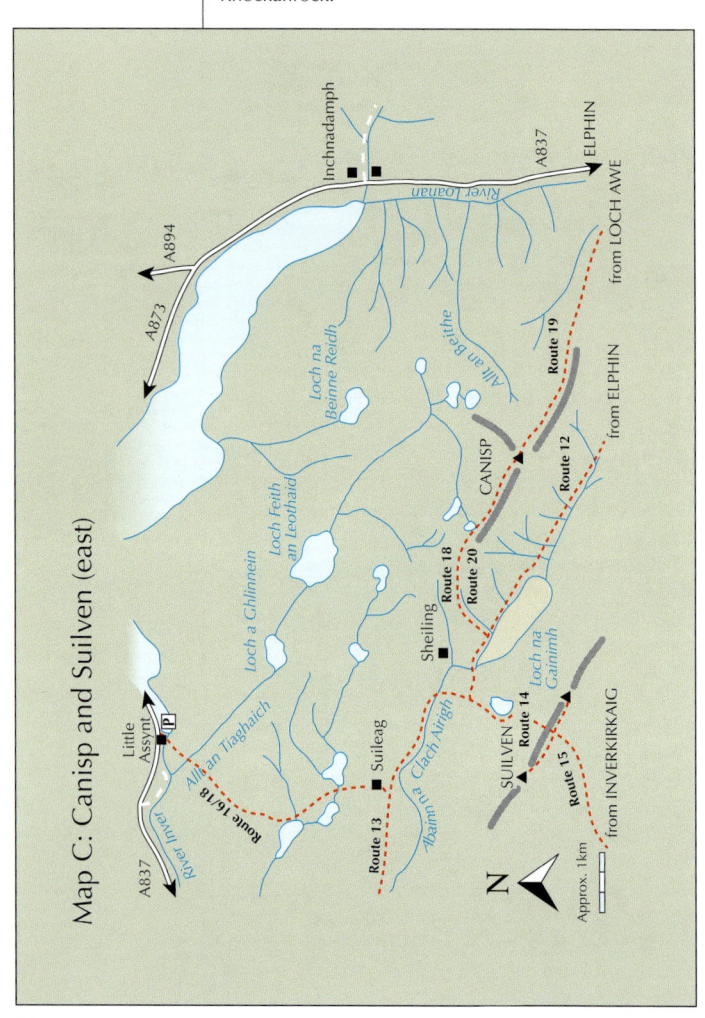

Map C: Canisp and Suilven (east)

Suilven, 731m (2398ft)

Suilven (at 731m) is a midget of a mountain even compared to its near neighbours Cul Beag, Cul Mor and Canisp, which are all Corbetts (peaks between 2500 and 3000ft). Yet despite this it manages to overshadow all of them. It is an extraordinary shape from any viewpoint. From the east it appears as a graceful spire backed by a bulkier dome; from the western seaboard it seems to be an isolated pillar – which is why the Vikings named it Sul Fjall ('the pillar mountain'). But when seen from the north or south its long and serrated ridge is prominent, and this aspect of the mountain was well described by W.H. Murray in his *Companion Guide to The West Highlands of Scotland* as resembling 'some high-decked galleon riding the seas of gneiss'.

While, like many Scottish mountains, the reality of the climb may not match its visual appeal, Suilven cannot be ignored.

Route 12: Suilven approach from Elphin

Distance:	22km
Height gain:	396m to foot of main ascent path and return)
Maps:	C, D
OS Map:	Landranger 15

The OS Landranger map shows the Elphin to Lochinver path departing the A835 road adjacent to the bridge over the Ledmore River and traversing a low hillock to reach the eastern end of Cam Loch. This path has been abandoned and is no longer distinct on the ground. A newer alternative path (still rather indistinct) leaves the road from a gate 300m east of the bridge, where there is parking for two or three cars, to miss out the hillock and join the old track as it leaves the loch shore.

Now quite distinct, the path initially heads north away from the loch, but soon bends right and returns to the loch shore. After following the shoreline closely for

1.6km (1 mile) or so, a long, gentle ascent to the north leads away from Cam Loch to reach Lochan Fada, hemmed in between Suilven's long south-east ridge and the mass of Canisp. Threading its way along the narrow valley of the Allt Ghlinne Dhorcha, the path emerges into more open terrain by the beaches of Loch na Gainimh.

At the far end of the loch, a footbridge is crossed and, soon afterwards a junction of paths with a small cairn is reached. From this point, follow the ascent description below (Route 14).

Route 13: Suilven approach from Lochinver

Distance:	19km
Height gain:	244m to foot of main ascent path and return
Maps:	C, D
OS Map:	Landranger 15

The route to Suilven leaves Lochinver by the road to Glencanisp Lodge (signpost 'Footpath to Elphin 14 miles'), which is at the southern end of the waterfront near to the Culag Bridge and the road to Inverkirkaig. The road climbs to a small parking area near to Loch Druim Suardalain with a sign requesting all vehicles to be left there. At the lodge, a further notice forbids the use of bicycles on the footpath, so from this point on it's feet only.

A good gravely path continues from the lodge, heading purposefully over a bumpy gneiss moor to reach a fork in the path. The left branch here leads to the bothy of Suileag, which is maintained by the Assynt estate.

From the Suileag path junction the main path continues as a broad and stony track, skirting the shore of Lochan Buidhe to a good footbridge over the Abhainn na Clach Airigh. From here it swings south and begins to climb up above the stream towards the outlet of Loch na Gainimh, where there is a second footbridge. About halfway between the two bridges, a cairn on the right (south-west) of the path announces the start of the route to the Bealach Mor in the middle of Suilven's main ridge. From this point, follow the ascent description in Route 14.

Route 14: Suilven ascent from the north-east – main ascent path

Distance:	6.5km
Height gain:	580m
Maps:	C, D
OS Map:	Landranger 15

Now it's time to don your best bog-slogging gear and tackle the sliding heap of ooze which passes for Suilven's lower slopes. The initial pull up leads to a scramble up an escarpment of heather, loose stones and peat, which brings you to the shore of the well-named Loch a Choire Dhuibh ('loch of the black corrie'). This bog-encircled pool is skirted on its north-west shore to reach drier and rockier slopes at the foot of the Bealach Mor gully. The path up the gully is steep and loose, especially at the top, but it leads without further difficulty to the narrow col at the centre of this wasp-waisted mountain's mile-long summit ridge.

Route 15: Suilven ascent from Inverkirkaig

Distance:	22km
Height gain:	762m
Maps:	C, D
OS Map:	Landranger 15

The Inverkirkaig route starts from a car park where the Baddagyle to Lochinver road crosses the River Kirkaig. There is a café and a bookshop here, and the popular path to the Falls of Kirkaig provides the initial approach to Suilven.

Starting from the car park, a pleasant path leads up through sylvan woods. Gradients are easy, and the surface

WALKING IN SCOTLAND'S FAR NORTH

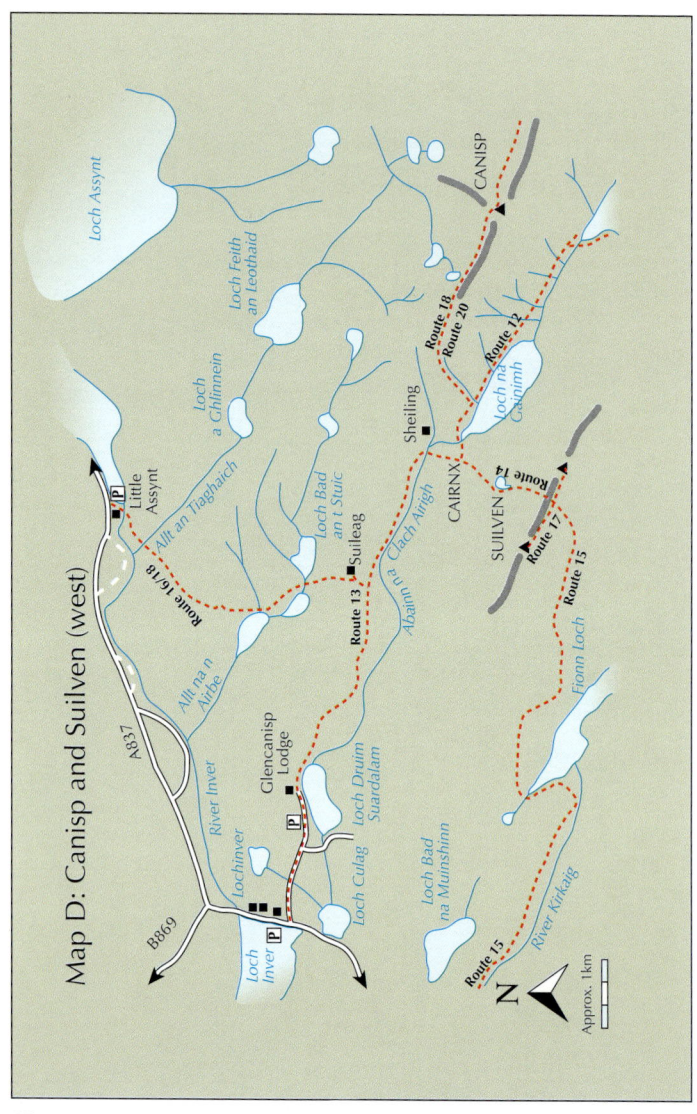

Map D: Canisp and Suilven (west)

Route 15: Suilven ascent from Inverkirkaig

underfoot pleasant and gravelly. The path initially stays close to the river, but eventually begins a climb away from it, rising onto broad slopes high above the valley to eventually arrive above the falls. The falls themselves are not visible from the path, and if continuing direct to Suilven will not be seen.

If you want to see the falls you have to descend an initally boggy path (a cairn marks the junction) which gets steeper, leading down to a series of eroded rocky/earthy steps (unpleasant in the wet) in view of the falls. Although not particularly high – no more than 15m (50ft) – the setting and the volume of water make the Falls of Kirkaig worthy of the detour.

Back on the main path, continue in the upstream direction for a further 500m until opposite a prominent set of rapids. A cairn here marks the start of a short-cut path, which leads across a boggy spur to the shore of Fionn Loch.

In clear weather Suilven is now well in view, but looks (and is) surprisingly distant. The path, still distinct and mostly fairly dry, skirts the south-west shore of the loch, then loops north and east to return around the opposite shore. After crossing a broad, flat-bottomed corrie (Coire Mor) a shallow valley leads up to a col with a small cairn, from where the path can be seen continuing down to the loch again. Leave the main path here and follow a smaller one, heading initially east, which climbs precariously across a craggy slope to emerge on a sloping plateau below the towering south-west face of Caisteal Liath.

From this point, the path becomes wetter and less distinct, but cairns act as a guide across these broad lower slopes and lead to the foot of the final climb.

As the mountain proper is approached, the path dries out and climbs purposefully up towards the Bealach Mor (a central col), which provides the only chink in Suilven's armour on this side as well as on the north-east side. The path is very eroded and gets worse as height is gained, the last few feet to the Bealach being quite a struggle – especially in bad weather.

In comparision to the gully on the opposite side of the Bealach Mor, I would say that this side is easier and less unpleasant until the last 35m (100ft), after which there is little to choose between them. Both have very steep and eroded finishes.

Route 16: Suilven approach from Little Assynt

Distance:	16km
Height gain:	457m to foot of main ascent path and return
Maps:	C, D
OS Map:	Landranger 15

This is a rougher alternative to those above, involving a burn-fording and only a thin and indistinct path in the early stages. It is, however, probably the shortest approach available.

To the east of the buildings of Little Assynt (GR155249), on the south side of the road, there is a lay-by with room for two cars (usually empty). Traces of a former stile will be found in the fence here, and a southerly beeline leads in 30m to a distinct path running south-west to a good footbridge over the River Inver, here sliding through a rocky little gorge. The path continues via a

Suileag bothy (photo: Andy Walmsley)

stile (surrounded by glutinous bog) to the crossing of the Allt an Tiaghaich, which can be problematic in times of spate. Normally a calf-deep crossing can be made and the path resumed as it crosses a low bealach (c.210m). The terrain consists of rough moorland, often wet, and the path is narrow but quite distinct.

After climbing gently for a while, the path descends through a broad basin containing three lochans and soon reaches the well-maintained bothy of Suileag (maintained by the Assynt estates). Keeping above the walled enclosure which is seen below the bothy, the path descends south-west to join the broad track from Glencanisp Lodge, from which point the descriptions of Route 13 and Route 14 above can be followed to the summit.

Route 17: Traverse of the Suilven summit ridge

Distance:	variable
Ascent:	variable
Maps:	C, D
OS Map:	Landranger 15

The summit ridge is generally less exciting than the mountain's appearance might suggest, and surprisingly ranks a poor second to Stack Polly's, although its loneliness has an appeal which is denied the latter mountain. The highest, western, summit (Caisteal Liath) has a broad grassy top with a brilliant view over Lochinver, and is easily reached from the col by a good path with no difficulties.

The opposite end of the ridge is more interesting, and the final (south-east) summit of the mountain, Meall Bhig, is reached only by some exposed manoeuvres. The difficulties and exposure are severe enough to make this end of the peak the preserve of those with real mountaineering experience. Rock climbers and inveterate scramblers will find it straightforward, but there are a number of delicate moves required above big drops, especially crossing and ascending from the final gap. This route is therefore outside the scope of this guide.

Canisp, 846m (2776ft)

Canisp is an unfortunate peak. Being in close proximity to Suilven (one of the undisputed stars of the far north) it suffers from obscurity. Despite its considerable superiority in height, the mountain cannot compete with Suilven's jutting presence.

Canisp's case is not helped by the fact that it turns its most dowdy face toward the main road, thus ensuring that it is largely ignored. However, the hill is worth climbing (for Corbett-baggers it's compulsory), and those who approach it from the north-west will find that it has an excellent ridge and an altogether more imposing appearance on this side.

Route 18: Canisp ascent from Little Assynt

Distance:	26km
Height gain:	1158m
Maps:	C, D
OS Map:	Landranger 15

This is a longer, lonelier and more interesting route to Canisp than the 'normal' (direct) route from Loch Awe (Route 19). The approach is as for Suilven (Route 16), but instead of leaving the distinct Lochinver–Elphin path before Loch Na Gainimh, continue via a second footbridge to the loch side (see OS map). Below a craggy outcrop on your left, you will see a small burn tumbling down a shallow ravine with a path climbing by its west (true right) bank. Follow this path as it follows the stream purposefully upwards to peter out directly below Canisp's north-west ridge. The ridge is steep and well defined, and it makes a perfect route up the mountain, with great views across to Suilven on a clear day.

Route 19: Canisp ascent from Loch Awe

This is probably the most popular way to ascend Canisp, or at least the most commonly used. It is the easiest and

Route 20: Canisp to Suilven link route

Distance:	12km
Height gain:	700m
Map:	C
OS Map:	Landranger 15

has the most gentle gradients, but is without doubt the least interesting.

There are a couple of sizeable parking places on the A837 near Loch Awe, and small paths lead down to a footbridge at the outlet of the loch. From here, follow a line of small cairns; they will guide you towards the squat summit 'cone' of the hill over terrain consisting of mainly quite bare ground, with some scattered white stones and an occasional outcrop of living rock.

As the summit hump is approached, there are two possible route choices; either continue on the crest of the broad ridge, curving round in a more southerly arc to approach the top from the south, or continue on a bee-line for the summit. This latter option will lead you into a rising traverse on the north-east flank of the ridge, eventually reaching the head of a shallow stream gully, leaving a steeper final pull up to the summit.

The summit itself is an unremarkable stony plateau, but is well worth a visit on a clear day for the tremendous view of Suilven across the profound hollow containing Loch na Gainimh, its gashed summit ridge standing out spectacularly from here.

Route 20: Canisp to Suilven link route

Distance:	7km
Height gain:	579m summit to summit
Map:	C, D
OS Map:	Landranger 15

Suilven is an imposing object when seen from Canisp, and if the day is favourable, many will be tempted to add it to the itinerary. The route between the two peaks is quite

WALKING IN SCOTLAND'S FAR NORTH

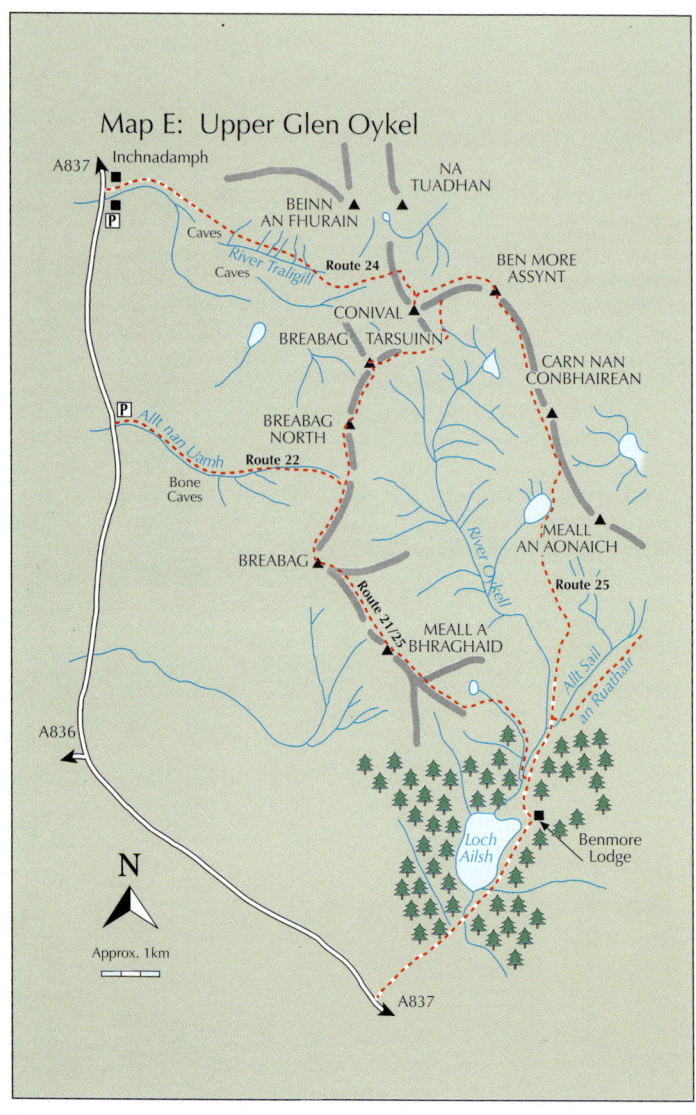

Map E: Upper Glen Oykel

Route 21: Breabag ascent from Benmore Lodge

straightforward, but it is not an easy option; there is arduous terrain and over 500m of ascent to overcome before the domed top of Caisteal Liath can be trodden.

Leave the top of Canisp in a north-westerly direction, soon picking up a well-defined ridge which gives good downhill walking towards a tiny lochan, nestling in a hollow slightly to the north of the mountain's main spine. Just before reaching this lochan the angle of the slope to the south-west begins to ease, allowing you to bear slightly left, crossing the headwaters of a small stream. Continue to descend in this direction (slightly south of west) to pick up a thin stalker's path which descends rather steeply to the shore of Loch na Gainimh, where Routes 12 and then 14 are followed to the summit.

Breabag, 800m (2625ft)

Although not a spectacular or impressively high peak, Breabag is a prominent object in the Assynt area, the vast slopes of white scree on its western face being prominent to any traveller approaching along the A835 from the south. The hill takes the form of a long whaleback ridge, stretching from Sgonnan Mor (overlooking Loch Ailsh and Benmore Lodge) to the narrow pass separating it from Conival. It bounds the whole of the western side of the upper Glen Oykel and forms one arm of the Oykel Horseshoe.

Route 21: Breabag ascent from Benmore Lodge

Distance:	14km
Height gain:	700m plus 5km each way from the road
Map:	E
OS Map:	Landranger 15

The only convenient approach to Breabag from the south is from Benmore Lodge, reversing the end of the Oykell Horseshoe (Route 25).

The initial climb from this end of the ridge is extremely steep and tiring, and the upper slopes very long and tedious. If the intention is to walk the Oykell Horseshoe in reverse this climb has to be done, but if the intention is to 'bag' Breabag the approach from Allt nan Uamh is much better.

Route 22: Breabag ascent from Allt nan Uamh

Distance:	12km
Height gain:	670m
Map:	E
OS Map:	Landranger 15

Where the Allt nan Uamh crosses the main A837 road (GR253179, spot height 138m on OS Landranger 15) there is a small car park. This is popular with educational groups, as it is the starting point for the walk to the 'bone caves', where prehistoric remains were discovered in 1917 by the geologists Peach and Horne. It is also a convenient starting point for Breabag.

Follow the main path upstream, passing a gushing spring where the stream from the upper valley re-emerges from the limestone, to a point immediately below the caves, which are seen high on the hillside to your right (south) at the foot of a beetling crag. The caves can be visited via a narrow branch path which leaves the main path shortly before this point.

From the valley immediately below the caves, a route choice presents itself. Ahead, the valley forks; it's the left fork which leads to the upper valley, but a waterfall (usually dry) bars an ascent via the stream bed, forcing a traverse above on exposed gravelly slopes. The alternative is to leave the valley bed at the caves and climb a steep grassy slope (traces of path) to cross a spur at a much higher level and regain the valley bed above the waterfall.

Now continue upstream, passing a succession of pretty cascades and small pools (very tempting on a hot day) to emerge in a marshy hollow under the main

Breabag ridge. A final steeper climb by the stream brings you to a tiny lochan close to the watershed, with the stony wastes of Breabag's northern summit visible to the north and easy grass slopes rising to the south.

Head south up these grass slopes, aiming for a gateway between two rocky outcrops. This opens into a curious grassy trough with rocky ridges on each side. This shallow trench, a useful guide in mist, leads unerringly to the final ridge and the highest point.

Route 23: Breabag to Conival link route

Distance:	7km
Height gain:	640m summit to summit
Map:	E
OS Map:	Landranger 15

This is rather a tough proposition and is actually better done in reverse (i.e. climb Conival and then bag Breabag). The problem is that the direct ridge route between the two peaks is barred by Conival's hostile south-west face. The craggy steepness of this face is not emphasised on the Landranger map, but standing on Breabag Tarsuinn (Breabag's northernmost top) you will be very much aware of it, as you stare this rocky acclivity straight in the face.

The key to the link is to skirt around the toe of Conival's tremendous south-eastern buttress into Garbh Coire, where you will be faced with almost 300m of scree leading up to the ridge between Conival and Ben More Assynt. This scree slope involves some serious hard labour, but will take you to the summit ridge without further difficulty.

Ben More Assynt, 998m (3274ft), and Conival, 984m (3228ft)

These two mountains are the highest in the old county of Sutherland, their imposing mass of gneiss and quartzite overtopping all the sandstone upstarts by some 150m (almost 500ft). Despite this, they are not prominent objects in the landscape, and Ben More particularly hides itself away behind lower outliers. At Inchnadamph, Conival's apron of whitish scree is well seen up Gleann Dubh, but the gaze is much more likely to be turned on Quinag's southern top (Spidean Coinnich), which towers majestically over the head of Loch Assynt with the ruin of Ardvreck Castle in the foreground. Once you have penetrated the inner sanctum of these mountains, though, you cannot fail to recognise their grandeur.

Route 24: Ben More Assynt and Conival ascent from Inchnadamph

Distance:	18km
Height gain:	1112m by described route
Map:	E
OS Map:	Landranger 15

Ben More Assynt, higher (by 14m) and more famous than Conival, is completely hidden away behind its lesser neighbour in the view up Gleann Dubh. The imposing scree-covered face seen from Inchnadamph is Conival's south-western flank.

The two peaks are actually two summits of the same mountain mass, and a very impressive mass it is too – the wild hollow of Garbh Coire at the very head of Glen Oykell being particularly impressive. The route described here takes in both summits and Ben More's entertaining south ridge, and includes a crossing of the floor of Garbh Coire beneath Conival's soaring south buttress. It is a fairly arduous outing, taking rather longer than might be imagined from a cursory glance at the map.

Start along the gravel road which passes in front of Inchnadamph Lodge (north side of River Traligill), and follow this as it curves south-east into the Traligill Glen (Gleann Dubh) to cross the river via a concrete ford. After passing a small croft house on the left, the path forks – the

ROUTE 24: BEN MORE ASSYNT AND CONIVAL ASCENT

right fork leads down to the river bed and the prehistoric caves of Traligill, but these can be visited on the return journey if desired. Take the left fork, climbing gradually uphill on a deteriorating path to pass through a small plantation. Emerging from this, the path (now very eroded and boggy) climbs just south of east to reach the obvious ravine to the west of Conival's broad slopes.

Having reached the ravine, the path turns steeply uphill to follow the watercourse, which descends in pretty waterfalls from the col between Beinn an Fhurain and Conival. Do not be tempted to make a beeline eastwards to the summit ridge, as the scree slopes are very unpleasant and the normal route is much more scenic.

At the head of the waterfalls the path meanders through a very attractive green hollow (great bivouac sites here!) before scrambling up an easy rock band to reach a col on the main ridge. Turning south, a rocky ridge, narrowing as it rises, leads to the summit cairn.

From here, Ben More Assynt looks unimpressive, appearing as two minor outcrops of rock at the end of a mile-long shattered ridge, and its extra height is not at all obvious; however, it is the 'great mountain of Assynt', so it must be visited. In any case, it has an airy south ridge which is well worth a visit.

The linking ridge is rough and seems longer than expected, but leads without difficulty to the higher top. Keep right (south) along the ridge to get the best views into Garbh Coire.

At the summit the ridge turns south, forming the eastern arm enclosing Garbh Coire. This south ridge is quite narrow and exciting. There are no major difficulties, but angled slabs form narrow sections on the crest in places. These are easy when dry, but could become increasingly difficult in wet, windy or wintry conditions. In good weather the traverse is an enjoyable sporting ridge walk.

At the end of the narrow section of the ridge a descent must be made to Dubh Loch Mor, but do not attempt this until just before the rise to Ben More Assynt's south summit (Carn nan Conbhairean on OS Landranger 15). At this point a shallow gully, with evidence of previous descenders, falls westward to reach the corrie floor just south of the loch. This gully is extremely steep, but has no other difficulties, though large parties should stay close together to minimise the danger of dislodged stones falling on those below. In winter conditions, the descent of Ben More Assynt by this route would require mountaineering skills and equipment.

From the foot of the gully, skirt the west shore of the loch amid grand mountain scenery and climb gradually north-west over peaty ground to reach the Breabag/Conival divide. This bealach forms a narrow grassy trench, with the huge walls of Conival to the north-east and the gentler (but still rocky) slope of Breabag Tarsuinn to the south-west. Passing through the bealach a good path will be picked up, and this leads purposefully down into the head of Gleann Dubh.

The path keeps close to the River Traligill as it meanders through the glen, and it is quite convenient to visit the prehistoric caves in the lower valley en route back to Inchnadamph.

Route 25: The Oykell Horseshoe from Kinlochailsh

Distance:	34km
Height gain:	1448m from A837
Map:	E
OS Map:	Landranger 15

The horseshoe of mountains surrounding the head of Glen Oykell make a grand cirque, and the Oykell Hoseshoe is a hill walk of the highest calibre. The only thing which detracts from the enjoyment of the route is the fact that the Benmore Lodge estate does not allow vehicles to drive up the track from the A837. This adds at least 10km (5km each way) of rather dreary track to an already tough walk, and puts the route out of the reach of all but the toughest and fittest walkers.

If you fall into that category, start from the A837 at GR296083 (parking on roadside verges nearby – do not

Route 25: The Oykell Horseshoe from Kinlochailsh

The head of Glen Oykell (Dubh Loch Mor and Garbh Coire) (photo: Tim Kelly)

use passing places) and walk along the gravelled track to Benmore Lodge. This is actually the start of a path which skirts right around the east side of the long ridge of Ben More Assynt, Beinn Fhurain, Beinn Uidhe and Glasven. After passing above the Eas a Chual Aluinn waterfall it crosses the Bealach a Bhuiridh to emerge at Loch na Gainmhich on the Unapool/Kylesku road – a long and interesting excursion through wild terrain.

From Benmore Lodge, continue along the track through a forested valley to a junction of streams. The more interesting route heads north from here, climbing steeply up onto the ridge of Sail an Ruathair to reach the deeply enclosed Dubh Loch Beag. It is possible to visit Meall an Aonaich in a short detour from here, but the diversion has little to recommend it.

Continue in a northerly direction from Dubh Loch Beag, climbing the straightforward slope of Carn nan Conbhairean to gain the crest of Ben More Assynt's south ridge. The ridge now leads via some exciting airy slabs to the main summit of the mountain amid true mountain terrain and scenery.

The ridge heading west from here is mostly composed of shattered boulders, but involves only a moderate amount of ascent and leads quickly to the summit of Conival, where the main spine of the range twists abruptly northwards. This is not the direction you want to follow to continue around the Oykell skyline, but it is equally obvious that a direct line south-west towards Breabag is impractical on account of big crags. The key is to retrace your steps towards Ben More Assynt for 500m to reach the head of a broad scree slope leading down into Garbh Coire. The scree is steep and rough, but leads down to easy ground in the coire, from where you can skirt around the foot of the crag to a narrow col separating Conival from Breabag.

Now climb a stony ridge, slightly south of west, to emerge on the summit of Breabag Tarsuinn (625m), most northerly top of the extensive Breabag massif. The broad and stony wastes of Breabag are not as bold and challenging as the peaks just traversed, but they afford rough mountain walking away from the crowds which can afflict the Ben More massif on some weekends.

Follow the increasingly rocky ridge south as it gently swells to the 715m summit of Breabag North and continue down easy slopes to a wide saddle with a small lochan where Route 22 is joined. The main summit at 800m is soon reached from here.

The descent begins in a south-westerly direction over featureless slopes strewn with stones (good navigation needed in mist). Aim for the subsidiary shoulder of Meall Diamhain and the narrow trough of the Bealach Choinnich just beyond. There is a tough little climb out of the bealach to gain the final ridge of Meall a Bhraghaid, but easy walking then leads to the fine promontory of Sgonnan Mor, overlooking Loch Ailsh and Benmore Lodge.

Now you need to negotiate a steep and rough descent eastwards to reach the stream issuing from Loch Coire na Meidhe. This stream provides the easiest route down to a footbridge near Benmore Lodge and the long track back to the A837.

Glas Bheinn, 776m (2546ft), and Beinn Uidhe, 740m (2428ft)

From most viewpoints, Glas Bheinn (Glasven) and Beinn Uidhe (Ben Uie) hardly catch the eye. They both take the form of long scree-covered, whaleback ridges with little in the way of distinguishing features, but they do have the virtue of offering a wild and lonely upland experience. Their crests (particularly the northern end of Glas Bheinn) give good high-level walking with tremendous views.

These two peaks, along with Beinn an Fhurain, also provide the link between Quinag and Conival on the long and arduous Assynt Horseshoe route.

Route 26: Glas Bheinn and Beinn Uidhe ascent from Loch na Gainmhich

Distance:	18km
Height gain:	853m
Map:	F
OS Map:	Landranger 15

Loch na Gainmhich (Ganvich) lies alongside the main A894 road, near the top of the pass between Skiag Bridge and Kylesku. As well as being a convenient starting point for Glas Bheinn, the loch also marks the start of a path to the celebrated waterfall of Eas a Chual Aluinn (sometimes spelt Eas Coul Aulin), which is Britain's highest, with a fall of some 200m (658ft). The route described here includes a visit to the waterfall on the return journey.

From the west shore of the loch (parking available at various points along this stretch of road), pick up a rough and muddy path which heads south along the flank of Glas Bheinn, climbing gently to a slight shoulder. Just before the path reaches its highest point, leave it and strike directly up the steep western slope of the mountain. A shallow grassy streak (visible from the main road – weather permitting) gives a surprisingly easy climb onto

WALKING IN SCOTLAND'S FAR NORTH

Glas Bheinn's north-west ridge, which then leads pleasantly up to the boulder fields of the summit plateau. The cairn is prominent atop a jumble of rocks, but it could

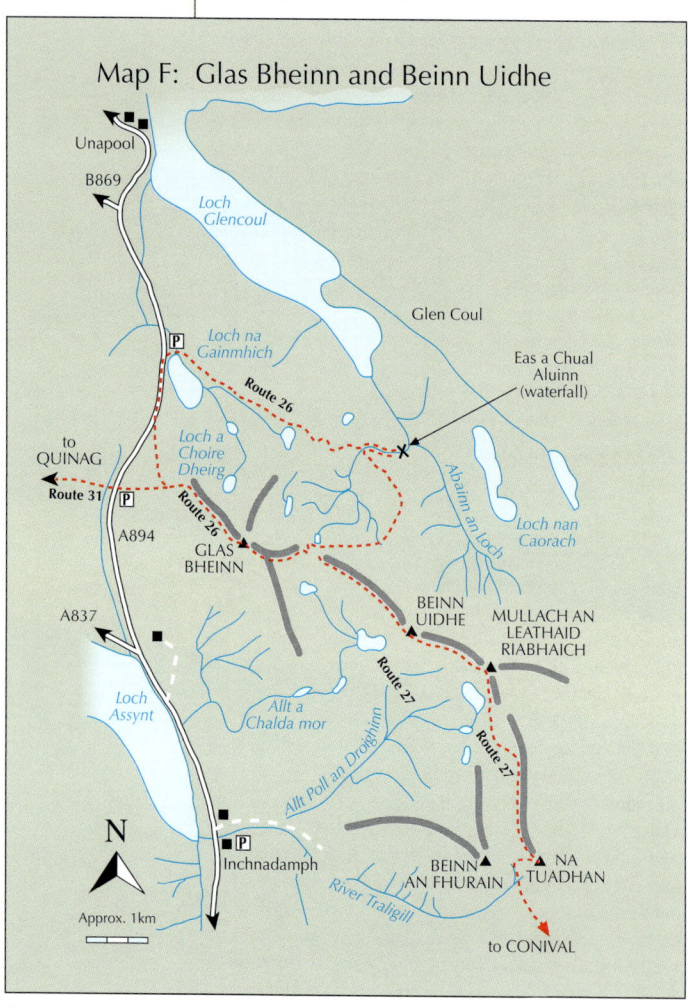

Map F: Glas Bheinn and Beinn Uidhe

ROUTE 26: GLAS BHEINN AND BEINN UIDHE ASCENT

prove difficult to locate in mist as the surrounding terrain is broad and featureless.

Leaving the summit, the edge of the north-eastern escarpment provides a handrail in mist (and good views in clear weather), leading to a distinct path which materialises as the ridge narrows and curves east to descend to a broad col (with cairn). This col separates Glas Bheinn from Beinn Uidhe and carries a path from Inchnadamph over the ridge into the rough hinterland above Glen Coul.

Beinn Uidhe is reached from the col along an easy-angled ridge, covered with a jumble of rocks. The path is invisible (no path can survive on this terrain), but the way is obvious, and the cairn, near the edge of the south-west slope, is soon reached.

Returning to the Glas Bheinn/Uidhe col, descend north-eastwards to a small lochan in a flat-bottomed corrie. A path is marked on the OS Landranger (Sheet 15), but this is sketchy and quite difficult to locate and follow. Instead, head east from the lochan, gradually curving north across rough but not difficult country to eventually reach the path (here distinct and cairned) where it crosses the Eas a Chual Aluinn stream.

Boggy paths on each bank of the stream descend from here to the lip of the fall. The detour is well worthwhile as the fall is spectacular, but extreme care is necessary because the escarpment falls away in a series of peaty ledges which are not very secure. The best view is obtained from a point further east, where the slope eases sufficiently for a lower ledge in full view of the fall to be reached in comparative safety.

Suitably impressed (or scared), return to the junction with the main path and turn right (north-west). A long meandering climb on a good cairned path now leads up to the loch and Bealach a Bhuirich. The loch occupies a pleasant sheltered bowl below the bealach and offers an excellent opportunity for picnics, sunbathing and swimming on a sunny day. On a wet and misty day its appeal is rather more esoteric.

From here, a straightforward descent on a well-trodden path leads back to Loch na Gainmhich. It is worth turning aside at the outlet of the loch to have a look at the unnamed waterfall here (care needed on the crumbling peaty edge). It is a surprisingly big fall and would be celebrated if it were in the English Lake District, but it suffers obscurity because of the proximity of 'the big one' just over the Bealach a Bhuirich. A better view of the fall can be obtained by approaching from below; the road to Kylesku crosses the stream nearby (after a conspicuous double bend). From the stream crossing, a short clamber up a narrow ravine brings the fall into view.

Route 27: Beinn Uidhe to Conival/Ben Mor Assynt link route

Distance:	12km
Height gain:	701m summit to summit including intervening peaks
Map:	F
OS Map:	Landranger 15

If it is desired to visit Conival or Ben More Assynt, a link can be made by continuing south-east from the summit of Beinn Uidhe along a bouldery ridge. Stay high on the crest until north of Loch nan Cuaran to avoid the most unpleasant scree slopes, then head south to cross the col to the east of the loch. Continuing this southerly line, a broad and grassy slope leads up towards the insignificant summit of Beinn an Fhurain, but this is an unworthy objective. Instead, head south-east to pick up a much more interesting scarp edge overlooking the valley of the Garbh Allt, and follow this over subsidiary humps to the bold and rocky summit of Na Tuadhan (860m) on the edge of an impressive precipice.

Leaving this airy summit, return due west until easier ground allows a descent south to a tiny lochan (marked on the map but unnamed). Do not be tempted to descend directly from Na Tuadhan to this point, because the scree/boulder slope thus encountered will make you wish you hadn't. A short grassy rise south of the lochan will bring you to the main Inchnadamph to

Conival path, which is then the obvious route to the summit (see also Route 57).

Quinag, 808m (2651ft)

Quinag (Cuinneag) is a tremendous multi-peaked massif which shows distinctly different faces depending on the viewpoint. From the south, approaching by the A837 to Loch Assynt, the most prominent object is Spidean Coinich, which appears as a shapely flat-topped cone, and many visitors must have mistaken this for the summit of Quinag. In fact it is only the terminal peak of the south ridge and is some 44m lower than the main summit.

From the west, coming from Lochinver along the A837, the mountain displays a long ridge seamed with gullies and topped with a switchback skyline of tops and cols. This is the long ridge from Spidean Coinich to Sail Gorm, and the main summit is again hidden from view.

From the north, as you head south from the Duartmore Forest to Kylestrome, you are presented with

Quinag (Sail Garbh) from the east (photo: Andy Walmsley)

Map G: Quinag

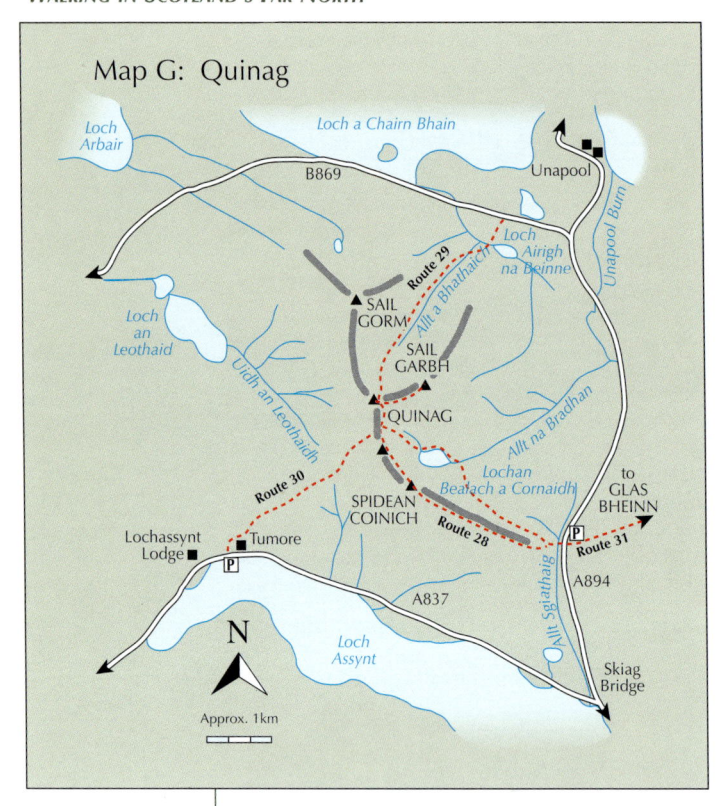

two distinct conical mountains towering above the Kylesku Bridge. These are the ends of Quinag's two most northerly ridges – Sail Garbh and Sail Gorm – with the former having the unusual 'barrel buttress' which gave the mountain its name (Cuinneag = 'milk jug').

Only from the east, as the A894 climbs from Kylesku towards Loch na Gainmhich, does the mountain display its true summit. The highest point crowns a massive wall of scree and grass which dominates the view of the hill from this side. Even though Spidean Coinich is in full view also, its true stature is more apparent from here.

Route 28: Ascent of Quinag from the East

Quinag is one of the best-known mountains in the far north, and deservedly so; the traverse of all the tops on its Y-shaped ridge is a memorable outing.

Route 28: Ascent of Quinag from the east

Distance:	11km
Height gain:	732m
Map:	G
OS Map:	Landranger 15

The normal approach to Quinag from the east is via the broad slopes of Spidean Coinich. Coming from the south, as the highest point of the Skiag Bridge/Kylesku road is approached, a large parking space appears on the right side of the A894 road (GR232272). This provides a convenient starting point for the ascent.

Cross the road and pick up a good path heading north-west towards the mountain's main bulk. Don't stay with this path unless you intend to bypass Spidean to aim

The eastern approach to Quinag

directly for the main summit. This direct alternative is described below, but Spidean is really too good to miss.

Leave the path after a few metres and climb up onto the broad back of Spidean's south-east ridge. There is no path on the ridge, but the walking is easy on slabs of quartzite-covered rock. The escarpment on the right guides you up over a subsidiary bump and across a bouldery col to the foot of the final cone, where a good path suddenly materialises. A stiff final pull leads to the tilted slab forming the summit of Spidean.

On a clear day, the view from here is spectacular, with the coastline of the Stoer peninsula ringed with white surf, and the hinterland sprinkled with a multitude of tiny lochans. Directly below is a dizzying view down to the Lochan Bealach a Cornaidh – bright turquoise on a sunny day, brooding black if the sky is dull.

The exit from the summit is not at all obvious at first, but the path comes into view as the northern edge of the plateau is approached. Be careful not to stray too far left on the initial scree slope, and instead keep close to the eastern escarpment on your right. This will bring you down to a grassy col with a pool and then easily up to the peaked top (marked with spot height 713m on OS Landranger 15). A delightful, if rather eroded, ridge now leads down steeply into the Bealach a Chornaidh – a profound notch in the main ridge which almost severs Spidean Coinich from the main massif. The wind really howls through here on a bad day, and few will linger in such conditions.

A sandy path now climbs obliquely across the facing slope to reach the grassy top of the 'junction peak' at 745m, with the two arms of Quinag's Y-shape stretching out on each side of the deep corrie of Am Bhathaich. Care is needed when departing the junction peak in misty weather, as it is easy to be led onto a dead-end ridge heading due north. This looks insignificant on the map, but can easily be mistaken for the mountain's main ridge if visibility is really poor. By the time the mistake is realised, a sizeable re-ascent can be required to regain the correct route.

ROUTE 29: ASCENTS OF QUINAG FROM THE NORTH

The turreted ridge out to Sail Gorm can easily be visited if desired, but if heading for the main top leave the junction peak initially in an easterly direction, then curve north-east as the ground levels out. The main ridge is a jumble of boulders, rising at an easy angle to the summit. The brownish Torridon sandstone disappears suddenly as the top is approached and grey gneiss is encountered.

The summit has an OS trig point and a low wall shelter, but ranks a poor second to Spidean Coinich as a viewpoint. For a spectacular view of Kylesku and its bridge, walk 600m further along the ridge (descent and re-ascent is required!) to the top of the famous Barrel Buttress, which gave the mountain its name. The view from the top of this tremendous precipice is well worth the extra distance and climb.

Note: It is not practical to descend to Kylesku from either of the northern ridges, and it will be necessary to return over the main top to the junction peak to find a safe descent route. If returning to the parking place at GR232272 the alternative route described below makes a good choice.

> **Alternative (direct) route:** If time is too tight to allow the traverse of Spidean Coinich en route to Quinag, then this alternative allows you to reach the Bealach a Chornaidh very quickly from the road and also makes for a rapid escape route in bad weather.
>
> The path leaving the A894 (see the start of Route 28) becomes less distinct as it climbs, but can be followed all the way to the sandy shores of Lochan Bealach a Cornaidh, from where a straightforward climb leads up to the Bealach itself. The route to the summit is then as described above.

Route 29: Ascents of Quinag from the north

Distance:	10km
Height gain:	700m
Map:	G
OS Map:	Landranger 15

Quinag's northern summits, Sail Gorm and Sail Garbh

The only practical route from the north for walkers is from the Assynt Coast Road. Parking can be found near to the spot height at 118m on the Landranger map (GR221319) and a rough ascent made into the Am Bhathaich corrie. This is a steep and heathery climb – not an easy option – but it does give tremendous close-up views of the mountain's northern buttresses.

The corrie itself is an excellent example of a hanging valley and is an eerily enclosed place, surrounded by steep scree-covered walls. The only escape routes which are even moderately comfortable are at the head of the valley, where easier slopes and less scree allow a relatively unhindered passage onto the main ridge near the junction peak.

From here, the options described in Route 28 can be explored.

Route 30: Ascent of Quinag from Tumore

Distance:	8km
Height gain:	732m
Map:	G
OS Map:	Landranger 15

ROUTE 31: QUINAG TO GLAS BHEINN LINK ROUTE

Travelling along the A837 from Lochinver towards Skiag Bridge on a clear day, Quinag's western wall makes an imposing object. From Spidean Coinich's flat top a high skyline with notches and turrets stretches northwards for some 4km. Most of this length is composed of the lesser spur of Sail Gorm, the main ridge and summit being hidden behind, but its appearance is a challenge to anyone who savours a high-level ridge walk.

At GR184267 on the north shore of Loch Assynt is the small house of Tumore. Just to the west of the house is a roomy lay-by on the south side of the road (usually empty), and just opposite this is a gate giving access to a path. This is the way to Quinag. Curving around the back of the house, you will join the path marked on the OS Landranger map (Sheet 15).

This distinct path rises easily to a broad col (Bealach Leireag) directly below the intimidating slopes leading up to the Bealach a Chornaidh on the main ridge of the mountain. The Bealach a Chornaidh seems to cut deeply into the mountain when seen from the east, but from this side it is surprising how high the col is.

The path you are on leads on down Gleann Leireag to the coast road near Loch Nedd – a pleasant walk – but if Quinag is the objective leave the path here and head up to towards the main ridge. There is no path on these steep lower slopes, but one can be picked up at a higher level if you keep initially more to the right (south). A final slanting climb on this path will take you onto the Bealach a Chornaidh, where Route 28 is joined.

Route 31: Quinag to Glas Bheinn link route

Distance:	9km
Height gain:	533m summit to summit
Maps:	F, G
OS Map:	Landranger 15

The link route between these two peaks is not often used, but it is an essential part of the Assynt Horseshoe (Route

WALKING IN SCOTLAND'S FAR NORTH

57). Descend from Quinag either via Spidean Coinich (east ridge) or directly from the Bealach a Chornaidh to reach the car-parking area at GR232272. From here, strike north-east across rough country to reach a muddy path traversing the slopes of Glas Bheinn north to south. A direct ascent from here is possible for those who relish struggling upwards over loose stones and scree. However, a better idea is to follow the muddy path northwards for 500m to the foot of a shallow gully (virtually devoid of scree) which gives relatively easy passage onto the ridge and thence to the summit (see Route 26).

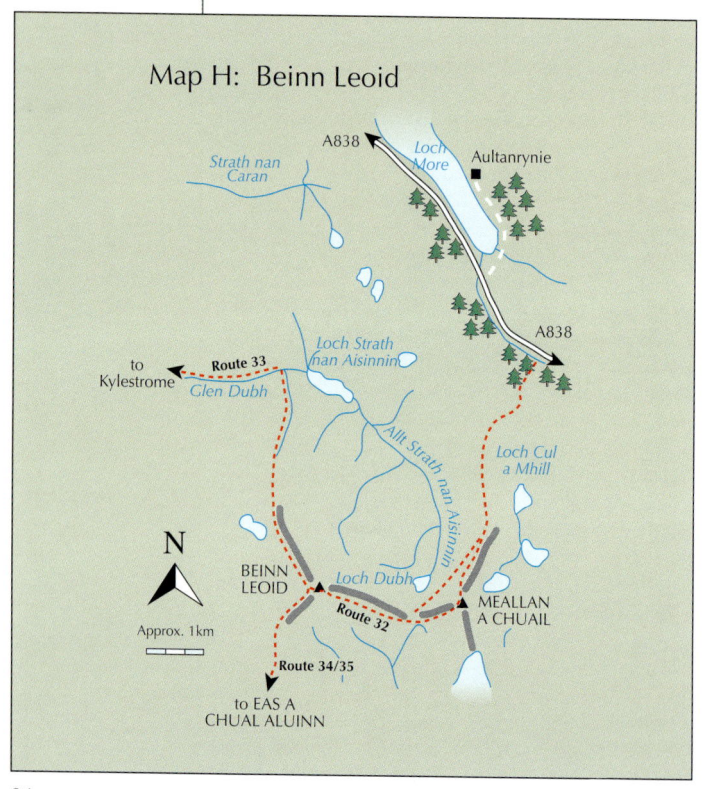

Map H: Beinn Leoid

Bein Leoid, 792m (2598ft), and Meallan A Chuail, 750m (2461ft)

These remote and lonely peaks are not prominently in view from any of the main roads in the district, hiding themselves away behind lower foothills. Beinn Leoid is visible from the vicinity of Kylesku, way off in the distance between the heads of Lochs Glencoul and Glendhu, but it is overshadowed by nearer peaks. However, both these hills are well worth the effort to reach them, and give a wilderness experience which can be somewhat lacking in other more populous areas.

Route 32: Ascent of Meallan a Chuail and Beinn Leoid from Kinloch, Loch More

Distance:	15km
Height gain:	1190m
Map:	H

The A838 road, from Lairg to Laxford Bridge, traverses the long shore of Loch Shin, then climbs gradually along the shore of Loch Merkland to reach a low col (the east/west watershed hereabouts) at 144m. This col takes the road over to Loch More, passing through a short narrow glen with plantations bounding the south side of the road. At GR357334 (marked with spot height 126m on Landranger 15) a path leaves the road to climb steeply up through a wide firebreak to the broad back of Meallan a Chuail's northern ridge (plenty of roadside parking). This is the most direct approach to both Meallan a Chuail and Beinn Leoid.

The path leads to the crest of the ridge, which is more like a moor at this point, and then becomes more indistinct as it descends to meet another path which has made a much longer crossing of the ridge from Lochmore side. Don't continue with the path. Instead, leave it at its highest section and head south over heathery moorland towards the narrower section of ridge which forms the summit of Meallan a Chuail.

The top is reached easily after a short final pull up, and the cairn is perched on the edge of a sizeable crag, giving superb views along the full length of Loch Shin.

Beinn Leoid's imposing bulk looms to the west, and it is a simple matter to make a beeline over reasonably easy terrain between the two peaks. However, don't forget that the ascent from the linking col to the top of Beinn Leoid is over 240m (800ft).

For the descent, return to the col, then either: use the distinct path heading down into the Allt Srath nan Aisinnin, leaving it at approximately GR340310 to climb back over the Chuail/Leitreach ridge, or contour Meallan a Chuail's north-west slopes to regain the crest of the ridge, in both cases descending by your outward path. Of these two alternatives, the latter is much better, as it involves less climbing and gives more open views.

Route 33: Ascent of Beinn Leoid from Kylestrome via Glen Dubh

Distance:	27km
Height gain:	853m
Map:	H
OS Map:	Landranger 15

This is a very arduous route. Distances are long, and the terrain can be trying. To reach the summit and return in one day is an outing for only the strongest of walkers, and only in summer. However, it does give a glimpse of the lonely hinterland surrounding the heads of Glen Dubh and Glen Coul, and would combine well with a wild camp or bivouac.

Parking in the vicinity of Kylestrome is now difficult. You may be able to find a space on the fragment of old road leading down to what was the ferry quay, but it may be easier to park on the large lay-by at the north side of the Kylesku Bridge and endure a little initial road walking.

Route 34: Ascent of Beinn Leoid and Meallan a Chuail

A number of paths leave Kylestrome. Take the one which hugs the shore, following this past picturesque waterfalls on the Maldie Burn and into the upper reaches of the fjord-like Loch Glendhu. The trek into the head of the valley is long and the path is rough, but eventually you enter the narrow defile of Glen Dubh.

After passing the plantations which cloak the lower slopes on the south side of the glen, a stream is seen cascading down the craggy slopes to the south. Follow this upward to a small lochan in a hollow of the shallow upper valley. From here, a line to the south-east leads you over rough slopes onto the end of Beinn Leoid's north-west ridge, which can then be followed (pathless) to the summit of the peak. Return by the same route.

> **Alternative return:** If you intend to incorporate a bivouac, an alternative return route would be to descend over the south-west summit into Glen Coul, cross the ridge of the Stack of Glencoul (tremendous views of Eas a Chual Aluinn – Britain's highest waterfall) to Loch Beag, then return along the southern shore of Loch Glencoul to Kylesku. The best bivouac/camp sites on this route are to be found near the head of Loch Beag, but the return by Loch Glencoul is no easy option. There is no path along the shore and the terrain is very rough. At one point, cliffs falling sheer into the loch bar progress, and the only alternative is to traverse a steep grass slope above the cliffs with considerable exposure. Do not undertake this expedition unless you are confident of your fitness, experience and resolve.

Route 34: Ascent of Beinn Leoid and Meallan a Chuail from Loch na Gainmhich via Eas a Chual Aluinn

Distance:	24km
Height gain:	1500m
Map:	H
OS Map:	Landranger 15

This route will not be suitable for all readers. To reach Beinn Leoid or Meallan a Chuail by this route and return within a day requires a high level of stamina and experience in Scottish wilderness walking. It involves a considerable amount of descent and re-ascent before the goal is reached, and includes a lot of rough, boggy, pathless terrain. However, it does make for a satisfying expedition, and could be tackled in a leisurely manner with a wild camp or bivouac near the Eas a Chual Aluinn or on the shore of Loch an Eircill.

The initial section of the route follows the main path to Eas a Chual Aluinn, described in Route 26, and gives an easy start to the walk. Once at the waterfall, continue along the escarpment edge (south-east) until the slope eases sufficiently to allow a descent to the bed of the Abhainn an Loch Bhig. The view of the 'splendid waterfall of Chual' from here is indeed splendid.

From the foot of the fall, climb rough and steep slopes north-east to attain the neck of land behind the summit of the Stack of Glencoul, which is easily visited, and worth the effort for the great view of Loch Glencoul and the waterfall opposite. Below you now is the head of Glen Coul, with a clearly visible path leading up to

Stack of Glencoul from Loch Glencoul

ROUTE 34: ASCENT OF BEINN LEOID AND MEALLAN A CHUAIL

Loch an Eircill. Make a diagonal descent to reach the outlet of the loch and pick up this path. Follow the path south-east to reach a sizeable tributary stream about halfway along the loch shore, and follow this stream uphill into a shallow valley to eventually emerge by a small lochan.

You are now within striking distance of Beinn Leoid; a direct climb due north up relatively easy slopes will bring you to the domed top of the mountain's western summit. The main summit is reached via an easy climb north-east.

To reach Beinn Leoid by this route and return will be quite enough for most people, but if one mountain in the day seems lazy (!), Meallan a Chuail is within easy reach. Follow the stony east ridge of Beinn Leoid down to a broad col, from where a stiff pull up will take you to the summit of Meallan a Chuail. To return from here, without having to climb Beinn Leoid a second time, which would surely be too much, descend to the col then bear left (roughly south-west) keeping to the same height and contouring across Beinn Leoid's southern slopes. A slight climb is necessary at one point to cross a broad outlying hump in the slope, and this brings you onto a broad shelf giving easy walking. Soon you cross a stream heading temptingly downhill. Do not follow this, as it leads to Loch nam Breac Mora. Instead, keep on at the same level until a second stream is encountered, flowing down to the little lochan above Loch an Eircill. From here it's a matter of retracing your outward steps back to Loch na Gainmhich, remembering that the climb up the escarpment by the Eas a Chual Aluinn will be a real tester at this stage of the expedition.

Alternative: As an alternative to the out-and-back option, a long (and even more gruelling) wilderness traverse could be devised by continuing from Beinn Leoid down into Glen Dubh (see Route 33) then walking out along that valley to Kylestrome. A convenient transport arrangement would be needed to link the two ends of the walk.

Route 35: Beinn Leoid to Beinn Uidhe link route

Distance:	14km
Height gain:	760m summit to summit
Map:	H
OS Map:	Landranger 15

This route might be used by those involved in a long traverse of the Assynt country from Loch More to Inchnadamph or Benmore Lodge. The link between these two peaks would be the crux of such a route, crossing, as it does, some of the wildest and least frequented terrain in the district.

From a perusal of the map, the best route would seem to be keep well to the east, descending to Gorm Loch Mor and then climbing up into Garbh Allt to reach the col between Beinn an Fhurain and Conival. This way is possible, but crosses some seriously wet and boggy ground. The huge basin of Gorm Loch Mor is also a bit dreary and uninspiring.

A better route pieces together parts of routes described elsewhere in this book. Briefly, descend to Loch an Eircill and cross to the Eas a Chual Aluinn waterfall (see Route 34), then ascend to the col between Beinn Uidhe and Glas Bheinn (cairned path, but see also Route 26). This is a much more interesting option.

THE FAR NORTH-WEST AND REAY FOREST

The far north-west has a subtly different character to the Assynt and Coigach areas. The peaks here are somehow wilder, with a remote feel to them, and the country in between is lonelier and less frequented. A large part of this farthest-flung corner of Britain is composed of Torridon sandstone, giving a smoother landscape than the bumpy gneiss found further south, with less heather, more grass and far fewer tarns sprinkling the scene.

The Cape Wrath headland itself is backed by an isolated moorland known as The Parph. Both 'parph' and 'wrath' are corrupted forms of the same Norse word, 'hvarf', meaning 'a turning point'. This corner of Scotland marked the point where Viking ships would turn south to wreak havoc on the west coast of northern Britain. The name Wrath, though, is an apt English name for the wild and rugged coastline of the cape.

The Parph moor provides good opportunities for the seeker of solitude, and it is often used as a training ground by the adventure centre at Skerricha. It is, however, devoid of any major interesting features and is thus rather neglected by most visitors.

The remainder of this north-western corner of Britain contains of some of the very best mountains to be found anywhere in the country. The Reay Forest hills – Foinaven, Arkle, Ben Stack, etc – need no introduction, and the area has a network of excellent paths meandering over cols between these wild and lonely peaks. All these paths are a joy to explore.

The best bases for exploration of the far north-west and Reay Forest are Scourie, Kinlochbervie and Durness.

Ben Stack, 721m (2365ft)

Whether approaching from the north-west along the A894 or from the south-east along the A838, Ben Stack presents an imposing pyramid, and it looms impressively over those travelling along the shore of Loch Stack. Although its modest height makes it an upstart in the company of grand peaks such as Arkle and Foinaven, it refuses to be overshadowed, and is a prominent object in the Reay area. It is a target of many tourist cameras

WALKING IN SCOTLAND'S FAR NORTH

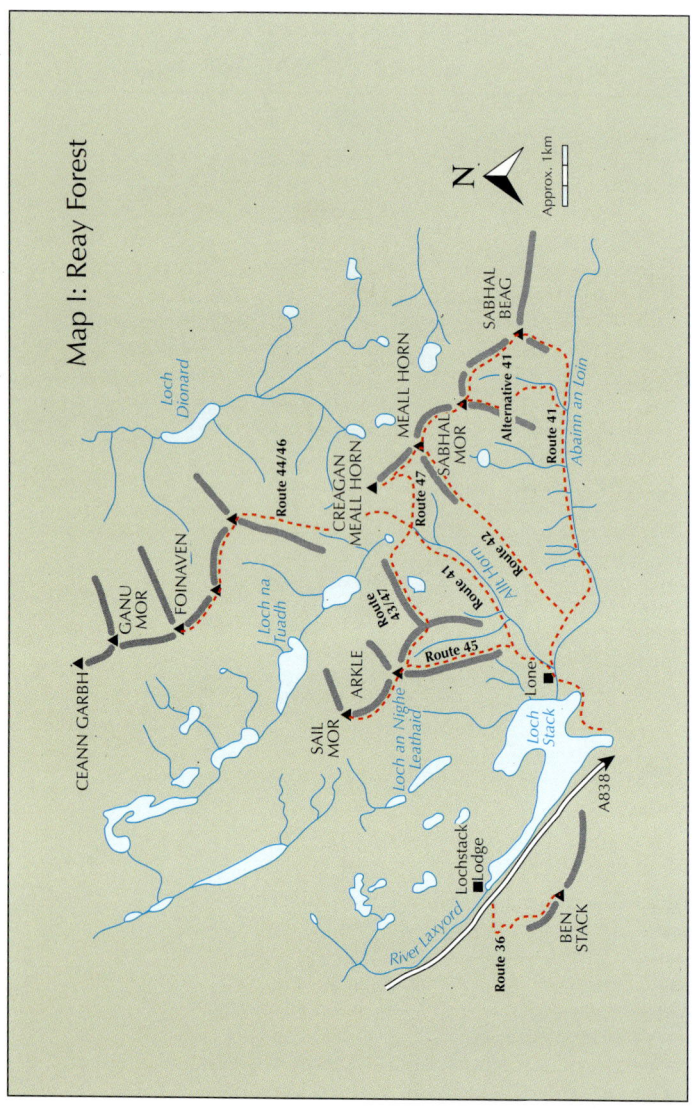

Map I: Reay Forest

Route 36: Ascent of Ben Stack from near Lochstack Lodge

and promises to provide a classic climb, which it does, if only on a small scale.

Ben Stack from Loch More (photo: Andy Walmsley)

Route 36: Ascent of Ben Stack from near Lochstack Lodge

Distance:	6km
Height gain:	670m
Map:	1
OS Map:	Landranger 9

Travelling between Laxford Bridge and Achfary, you will see a building on the right where the road passes between a plantation and the steep flank of Ben Stack (GR264437, about 5km from Laxford Bridge). There is parking for only two or three cars by the building, but there are alternative parking spaces not far away along the road. The ascent commences up a good track climbing diagonally westward from the road adjacent to the

Ben Stack and the River Laxford

building, and this gives easy progress to Loch na Seilge, from where a faint but cairned path heads directly up Ben Stack's north-west ridge, soon reaching a shallow col below the main summit pyramid.

A more direct line to this col is possible by leaving the initial track as it swings around a shallow little corrie (GR260436) and making a rising traverse south-east over steep grass and heather to arrive below the steep final ridge.

The path becomes much more distinct on the summit pyramid as it winds its way up between small crags and rock steps. The only difficulty hereabouts is steepness, and the path reveals itself a few metres at a time as each band of rocks is surmounted, finally emerging on a narrow little crest which leads directly to the cairn.

The summit of the mountain is formed of two parallel ridges. The northern one (above) carries the cairn on the highest point, along with a small transmitter station, while the southern one has the trig point. A shallow grassy trench separates them.

ROUTE 37: ASCENT OF BEN HEE FROM WEST MERKLAND

Alternative ascent: This ascent from Achfary via the Leathad na Stioma is less steep and offers more route choice, including a sporting little rock staircase, but it is longer and less interesting than the route described above and is best used as a descent route for those who wish to traverse the mountain. Note: The road along the shore of Loch Stack is not such a chore as might be imagined, as it carries very little traffic most of the time, has good views and rounds off a traverse of Ben Stack quite nicely.

Alternative: For those who will not endure road walking at any price, there is an alternative. Ascend the hill from Achfary via Leathad na Stioma, traverse the summit ridge and descend the upper, rocky, portion of the north-west ridge. At the first grassy col on the north-west ridge, turn sharply right and begin traversing back along the north-east face of the mountain. This initially rough traverse soon forms into a broad shelf which stretches all the way along this flank of Ben Stack and will lead you to a straightforward heathery slope overlooking the road near Achfary.

Ben Hee, 873m (2864ft)

Compared to many of the peaks in this guide, Ben Hee is a bit of a shapeless lump. It has no pinnacled summit, no swooping ridges, no rocky staircases and no imposing crags. The mountain hides its obese bulk away behind outliers to the north of Loch Merkland and does not throw down a challenge which says 'Climb me' in the way Suilven or Ben Stack does. It is not even a Munro.

There is only one good reason for anyone other than a dedicated Corbett-bagger to climb Ben Hee and that is the view. The ascent route described below is unexciting but tolerable, and saves the reward until the very last moment, when the summit is reached and the view northwards is revealed. It would be a shame to climb Ben Hee in cloudy weather; choose a day of spring or autumn sunshine, when the view is most extensive.

Route 37: Ascent of Ben Hee from West Merkland

Parking is available by the road to the west of the estate keeper's cottage at West Merkland (GR383329), and the

WALKING IN SCOTLAND'S FAR NORTH

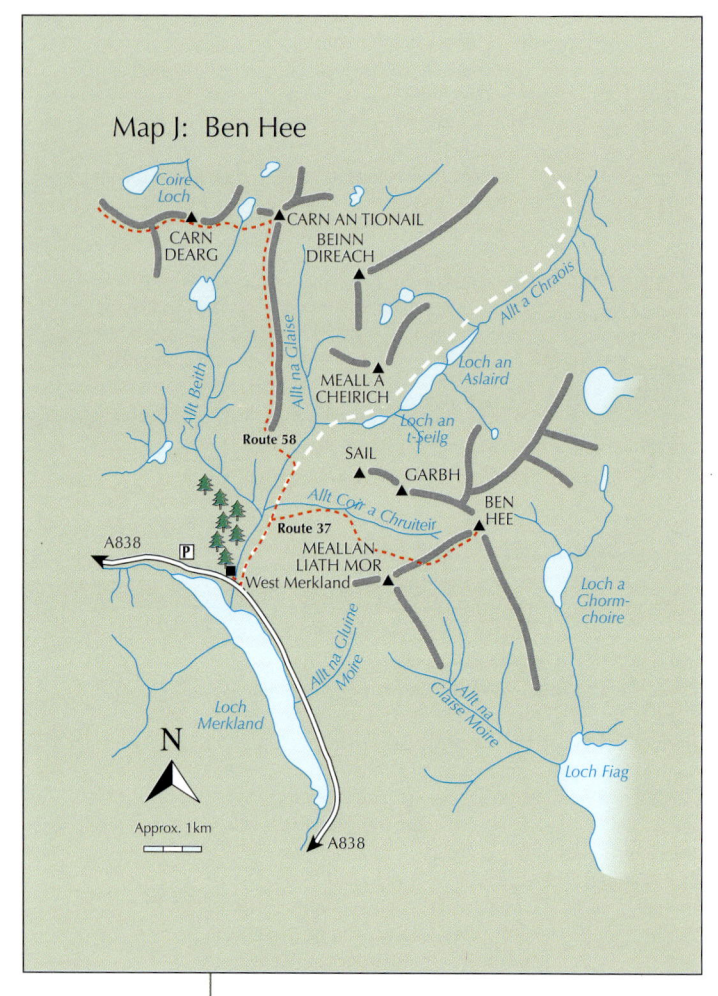

Map J: Ben Hee

route begins along a broad unsurfaced track (start of Bealach nan Meirleach) on the east side of the bridge by the cottage. The main gate is usually locked, but a smaller one is usually left open for the use of walkers.

ROUTE 37: ASCENT OF BEN HEE FROM WEST MERKLAND

Distance:	12km
Height gain:	790m
Map:	J
OS Map:	Landranger 16

The track winds easily upward through heather and eventually crosses the Allt Coir a Chruiteir, a small burn descending from the slopes of Ben Hee (about 1.5km from West Merkland). Just before reaching this stream, a low hump (too small to be called a knoll) with a bald patch appears on the right, with a tiny stalkers' path branching off through deep heather. This path improves as it makes its way up into the corrie, passing some pretty little waterfalls on the left.

After climbing through a narrow section, the path emerges into a wet hollow with a steep escarpment on the right, where it suddenly becomes indistinct. The direct line to the summit continues straight ahead to climb soggy slopes at the head of the corrie, but a better route exists. From the wet hollow, take a rock-strewn slope on the right, climbing south-west towards the broad saddle between Meallan Liath Mor and Ben Hee. This leads out onto easy, dry slopes, and a long plod over increasingly rocky ground northward brings the summit underfoot.

The view on a clear day is spectacular, with Ben Hope and Ben Loyal prominent in the north, Foinaven and Arkle north-westwards, and a fine skyline of the Assynt peaks to the west. If the day is exceptionally clear, the whole scene is perfectly framed by the vast blue Atlantic Ocean. Don't climb Ben Hee on a misty day!

> **Alternative:** There is a possible alternative route of descent. From the summit, descend easy slopes west-north-west to pick up the well-defined ridge of Sail Garbh, which bounds the northern side of the Alt Coire a Chrutier valley. A rough descent at the end of the ridge leads back to the Bealach nan Meirleach track and thence to your starting point – thus completing a kind of Ben Hee Horseshoe.

Meallan Liath Coire Mhic Dhughaill, 801m (2628ft)

The private estate road which leads from the A838 to the locked bothy of Lone is the key to a number of mountain ascents hereabouts, including Arkle, Foinaven, the Sabhals and Meall Horn, as well as Meallan Liath Coire Mhic Dhughaill. This latter mountain (whose name means 'the rounded grey hill of MacDougal's corrie') is one of the less frequented massifs of the Reay Forest but makes an excellent day out, with a number of subsidiary peaks and corries which are a joy to explore.

The hill is unfortunately positioned with regard to maps, being shared between three different OS Landranger sheets. The actual summit is on Sheet 15 (Loch Assynt), but the northern outliers are on Sheet 9 (Cape Wrath), while the eastern tops of Carn Dearg and Carn an Tionail (both worthy mountains in their own right) are on Sheet 16 (Lairg and Loch Shin). This makes it difficult to get a clear picture of the structure of the massif from the map, and could be a real pain if trying to navigate a route off it in mist.

Route 38: Ascent of Meallan Liath from Achfary via Lone

Distance:	13km
Height gain:	810m
Map:	K
OS Maps:	Landranger 9, 15, 16

The Lone estate road has a sign on the bridge saying 'No cars please'. So leave your vehicle by the bridge and walk the 3km in to the bothy, initially on tarmac, then on a stony Land Rover track.

Continuing, ignore a cairned junction with a branch to the left (the path to Arkle) and keep on along the right branch, which climbs over a shoulder to reach the valley

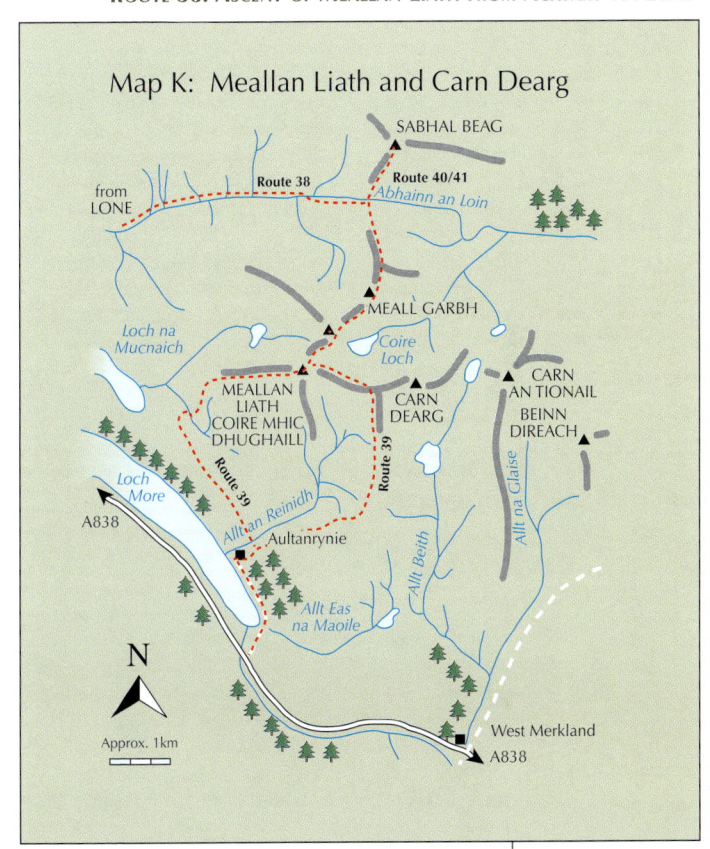

ROUTE 38: ASCENT OF MEALLAN LIATH FROM ACHFARY VIA LONE

Map K: Meallan Liath and Carn Dearg

of the Abhainn an Loin. Continue on a good vehicle track along the north bank of the stream for 3km to a final pull up which brings you to the top of the Bealach na Feithe.

Sabhal Beag lies to the north of this pass, up steep slopes, but to the south a pleasant ridge leads up over the summit of Meall Garbh (752m) and the north top (759m) to the main summit of Meallan Liath (801m). Descent by the outward route is easy but the walk out via Lone can be rather tedious.

Alternative: A better way to return to Achfary is to decend the stony west ridge to a broad shoulder with a small lochan (GR347390) and continue west-south-west, initially down steep rocky slopes then over heathery/boggy ground to reach the south-east corner of Loch na Mucnaich. From here head west, crossing a low ridge and making a descending traverse on rough slopes to the edge of a plantation on Loch More's northern shore. Skirting the plantation, you will reach the loch side, and a small path (uncomfortable in places) then leads along the bottom of Ben Screavie's crags. The scenery along here is tremendous. If the day is fine, Ben Stack appears impressively to the west, while if the weather is wet, a fine waterfall often appears, descending from Ben Screavie. The path continues distinctly round the western shore of the loch to emerge on the A838 road near Lochmore Lodge, 1km east of Achfary.

Route 39: Ascent of Meallan Liath from Aultanrynie

Distance:	18km
Height gain:	910m (including Carn Dearg)
Map:	K
OS Maps:	Landranger 15, 16

This is a rather more direct ascent than that described in Route 38, but the mountain does not show its best side to Loch More. To appreciate the structure of the massif it is better to climb it from the north. However, this route can be accomplished in 3 or 4 hours with reasonable fitness, so could serve as a half-day outing. Parking places can be found by the roadside to the south of Kinloch cottage and the Aultanrynie access track at the south-east end of Loch More.

Follow the track around the end of the loch to Aultanrynie, turning right just before the buildings onto a path which climbs determinedly up the steep spur south of the Allt an Reinidh ravine. Within 100m a fork is reached. Take the left branch, which crosses the stream on a good vehicle bridge and heads diagonally up the slope ahead.

The track climbs at an easy angle, with good views over Loch More, and eventually reaches the north-western shoulder of Leac a Ghobhainn, where it makes a curling descent round to the south-east. A stream is crossed here, and a wooden ramp has been built to aid the exit of vehicles from the ford, but the track almost immediately becomes indistinct in heathery terrain. A beeline to the north-east from here will bring you onto the steep skirts of the peak, and an obvious stream can be followed upwards to a small lochan on a broad shelf (GR347390). The western ridge of the mountain is now the obvious way to the top. Its lower part is broad, with easy rock bands to interrupt progress or add interest, but the ridge becomes better defined as height is gained and eventually leads out onto the easy promenade of the summit.

The recommended descent route continues along the ridge as it twists east and south-east to the west shoulder of Carn Dearg (the summit is easily visited from here if desired). Leave the ridge at this point (GR370387) and descend southward down an obvious spur to a tiny lochan on the ridge of Meallan Liath Beag. An easy walk along this undulating ridge now leads to a good path which winds its way easily down to Aultanrynie.

Alternative: A more direct return can be made by descending steeply from the main summit in a southerly direction and crossing a boggy plateau to the flat hump of Meall Reinidh. Contour this minor top on its eastern side and go down the steep slope below to reach the outward path just above Aultanrynie.

This alternative is recommended only in clear weather, as it is all too easy in mist to be lured into the Allt an Reinidh stream system. The lower ravine is narrow, steep-sided and has a series of waterfalls. It is very picturesque but makes an uncomfortable descent. The slope below Meall Reinidh is steep and uncomfortable at the best of times, but is less arduous than the ravine.

Route 40: Meallan Liath to Sabhal Beag (Meall Horn massif) link route

This route is unlikely to be done except by those engaged in a traverse of the Abhainn an Loin skyline, but it is included here as the only convenient link between the Sahals/Meall Horn massif and the Meallan Liath Coire MhicDhughaill massif.

Distance:	6km
Height gain:	533m summit to summit including intervening tops
Map:	K
OS Maps:	Landranger 9, 15, 16

From the summit of Meallan Liath, follow the ridge north-east to a subsidiary top (759m) and continue in the same direction, descending to a pronounced col and then climbing to the top of Meall Garbh. The ridge is less definite from here on, but the line down to the Bealach na Feithe is fairly obvious.

Continue ahead up a steep slope, initially grassy and later with rocky bands. There are traces of paths in places but none is continuous; it is better to simply climb straight up. Gradually, the slope eases and eventually gives way to the bald summit plateau of Sabhal Beag.

There may be some difficulty locating the highest point in mist as it is marked by only the poorest of cairns, but its height of 729m makes it 26m higher than its neighbour Sabhal Mor.

Meall Horn (Meall a Chuirn) and The Sabhals

Meall Horn, 777m (2549ft), **Sabhal Mor**, 703m (2306ft), and **Sabhal Beag**, 729m (2392ft), form a group of grassy hills unfairly ignored by most visitors to the Reay Forest, being overshadowed by the more famous peaks of Arkle, Foinaven and the upstart Ben Stack. It is true that the latter three peaks are much more impressive to look at, but the Meal Horn groups give good walking, great views over the lonely hinterland at the head of Strath Dionard and (usually) complete solitude.

Route 41: Ascent of Meall Horn and The Sabhals from Achfary via Lone

Follow the estate road to Lone and the path along the Abhainn an Loin to Bealach na Feithe (as described in

ROUTE 41: ASCENT OF MEALL HORN AND THE SABHALS FROM ACHFARY

Distance:	24km
Height gain:	1005m
Map:	1
OS Map:	Landranger 9

Route 38). From here, a stiff climb up a grass slope with occasional rock bands brings you onto the stony upper slopes of Sabhal Beag (the higher of the two Sabhals). Easy walking over a bald plateau leads to an easy descent to the broad col separating the two peaks, and Sabhal Mor is gained after a moderate pull up a broad spur.

The ridge is now obvious, curving north-west over stones followed by grass to the summit of Meall Horn (cairn). Keep to the northern edge of the ridge from here to enjoy striking views down to the corries of Lochan Ulbha and An Dubh Loch. The path from Lone, heading across into Glen Golly and Gobernuisgach Lodge, is prominently in view from here.

The last top on the ridge, Creagan Meall Horn, is reached after an easy climb up a stony slope. Walk to the north-west end of the ridge for the best view of Arkle and Foinaven, separated by a profound gulf, their screes dazzling white on a sunny day.

Crags ringing three sides of the summit bar a direct descent westward. Instead, return towards Meall Horn and curve down to the right just before the col. Rocky terraces are encountered, but these are easily descended or turned on the left (south). Head west to pick up the gravelled track back to Lone down the Allt Horn valley.

Alternative: If a slightly shorter walk is required Sabhal Beag can be omitted. Follow the route described above, but where the path begins to climb from the Abhainn an Loin to the Bealach na Feithe, leave it and head north. A stream descends from the corrie separating Sabhal Mor from Sabhal Beag, and this can be followed up until the slope eases, near a small lochan (GR362429). Skirt the lochan on its south side and mount north-west onto Sabhal Mor's southern ridge. This is a mild climb, and brings the summit underfoot quite easily. The route above can then be joined for the traverse of Meall Horn.

Route 42: Direct Ascent of Meall Horn from Lone

Distance:	13km
Height gain:	792m
Map:	1
OS Map:	Landranger 9

Meall Horn has a convenient spur, named as Creachan Thormaid on OS Landranger 9, which connects it directly with Lone. Its lower part is ill-defined and tedious, but it improves as height is gained.

Follow the path from Lone as if heading for the Abhainn an Loin, but leave it after the first steep little climb through a rocky gap. Head initially north from here up wet slopes of heather and grass, but gradually curve north-east as height is gained, climbing a steepening slope to the broad whaleback of Creachan Thormaid. The walking now improves and leads easily to a narrower 'neck' below the final 200m pull to the summit of Meall Horn.

Route 43: Meall Horn/Creagan Meall Horn col to Arkle link route

Distance:	8km
Height gain:	457m summit to summit
Map:	1
OS Map:	Landranger 9

A tough crossing, to be attempted only by those who still have a massive surplus of energy after completing the Sabhals/Meall Horn traverse.

Descend from the Meall Horn/Creagan Meall Horn col as described in Route 41 then head west, passing to the south of a small lochan (GR335452) to reach a scarp edge overlooking Loch an Easain Uaine. Now climb an increasingly stony ridge with tremendous views into An Garbh Coire, passing the minor outlier of Meall Aonghais to reach the south summit of Arkle (757m).

Route 44: Meall Horn/Creagan Meall Horn col to Foinaven

Refer to Route 45 for a description of the traverse of the summit ridge to the main top (787m).

Route 44: Meall Horn/Creagan Meall Horn col to Foinaven link route

Distance:	9km
Height gain:	700m summit to summit including intervening tops
Map:	1
OS Map:	Landranger 9

This is even tougher than the Arkle link (Route 43) and only recommended if you have plenty of daylight left or transport waiting – at Gualin House, for example.

Descend from the Meall Horn/Creagan Meall Horn col as described in Route 41, then turn right to ascend the main path to its highest point below Creagan Meall Horn. It may be possible to make a more direct line to this pass from the summit of Creagan Meall Horn, and the map makes it look decidedly tempting, but this side of the summit is girt with crags, and only experienced mountaineers should consider this alternative.

From the col, an easy-angled but tedious slope climbs 250m to Foinaven's southernmost top (c.770m), and a broad easy ridge leads onwards to the 806m top overlooking the Cadha na Beucaich 'pass'. The traverse of the summit ridge in the opposite direction is described under Route 48.

Arkle (Arcuil), 787m (2582ft)

Arkle (Arcuil) is a prominent object in many views of the Reay Forest, rising impressively above the gneiss moors in a massive wall of white scree. Like its neighbour Foinaven, Arkle's screes can sometimes give the impression of a snow-covered peak – adding to its apparent stature. In most views, especially from the A838 road skirting its south-west and west sides, Arkle appears to be a broad, bulky mountain, and the summit is imagined to be an extensive domed plateau, but this is not the case. Hidden away on the eastern side of the hill is a huge corrie (Am Bathaich – 'the byre'), and the crest of the peak curls around the head of this, creating an impressive 1.6km (1 mile) summit ridge.

Route 45: Ascent of Arkle from Achfary

Distance:	17km
Height gain:	884m
Map:	I
OS Map:	Landranger 9

Just to the north of Achfary a side track leaves the A838 heading towards the scattered buildings at Airdachuillinn and the bothy at Lone. There is parking by the bridge near the beginning of this track (GR298402), vehicles being prohibited from continuing beyond the bridge without special permission.

The road continues from the bridge with a smooth tarmac surface, but this only lasts until Airdachuillinn then reverts to rough stones. At Lone the track becomes grassy and, shortly beyond, reaches a junction. Take the left

Arkle and Loch Stack

ROUTE 45: ASCENT OF ARKLE FROM ACHFARY

branch for Arkle, heading for a remarkable split boulder at the entrance to a small plantation.

The path begins to climb steeply now, soon rising clear of the trees to zig-zag up to the mouth of the upper Allt Horn valley. At around 180m altitude, the gradient eases and the path curves into the upper valley. In a further 40m, look for a small cairn and an indistinct path branching north through the heather (GR319430).

This path soon becomes easy to follow as it now heads straight for Arkle's south summit, keeping well away from the western crags which rim this southern ridge of the mountain. On the upper slopes, a grassy streak splits the generally stony slope, making for an easier passage to the first top.

On arriving at this first summit, the spectacular C-shaped main ridge can be seen curling north and east to the main top, with steep craggy slopes falling from it and forming the walls of Am Bathaich ('the byre') – an amazing flat-bottomed corrie.

Heading now north-west, the route makes a rough, stony descent to the col at the head of Am Bathaich before climbing an equally rough stony slope to the summit ridge. The final approach to Arkle's main peak is over a fairly narrow ridge, part of which is formed into a flat and fissured pavement. The narrowness of this ridge is a surprise after seeing the mountain's apparent bulk from the vicinity of Lock Stack. In fact the mountain is formed of a fine and delicate crescent-shaped spine enclosing Am Bathaich and gives a tremendous feeling of space all around.

The summit gives good views of both Ben Stack and Foinaven, and provides (on a clear day) a superb panorama of the coastal inlets of Lochs Inchard and Laxford.

Alternative: The ascent (or descent) could be made via a path which starts at Lochstack Lodge (GR269436) and curves around Arkle's west and northern slopes (prominently marked on the OS Landranger Sheet 9, Cape Wrath). This gives a more scenic approach than the Lone route, but the section below the summit entails the ascent or descent of the Sail Mor (north-west) face of the mountain, the upper section of which is exceptionally steep and rough.

Routes 46 and 47: Link routes from Arkle to Foinaven (10km/762m) and Meall Horn

Distance:	8km
Height gain:	442m
Map:	1
OS Map:	Landranger 9

The links to these two peaks are straightforward. For Foinaven, return to the south top of Arkle and continue along the ridge, passing over the subsidiary summit of Meall Aonghais to descend past Lochan na Faoileige to the two lochans which feed Lochan Easain Uaine and Loch Tuadh in the profound hollow between Arkle and Foinaven. From here, climb northwards along the rim of craggy slopes above Loch an Easain Uaine to reach the southern end of Foinaven's main ridge. The main path from Lone to Glen Golly will be seen climbing up the slopes of Creagan Meall Horn to your right (east) as you approach this slope, but there is no advantage to be gained by using it.

For Meall Horn, follow the above route to the two unnamed lochans, then head due east, crossing the Glen Golly path and threading a diagonal grassy line between rocky steps to emerge on the col which links Meall Horn with its craggier neighbour, Creagan Meall Horn. From here you can visit either peak easily – both provide unusual views of Foinaven (seen end-on) and Arkle.

Foinaven (Fionne Bheinn), 914m (2999ft)

Foinaven is a range of mountains. Its multiple peaks stretch for more than 5km (3 miles) from Ceann Garbh at the north-west end, over Ganu Mor (the highest top and almost a Munro) and six further tops to finally descend to a broad col, where it links up with the Meall Horn group. Swooping ridges – a joy to walk on – link all these

FOINAVEN (FIONNE BHEINN)

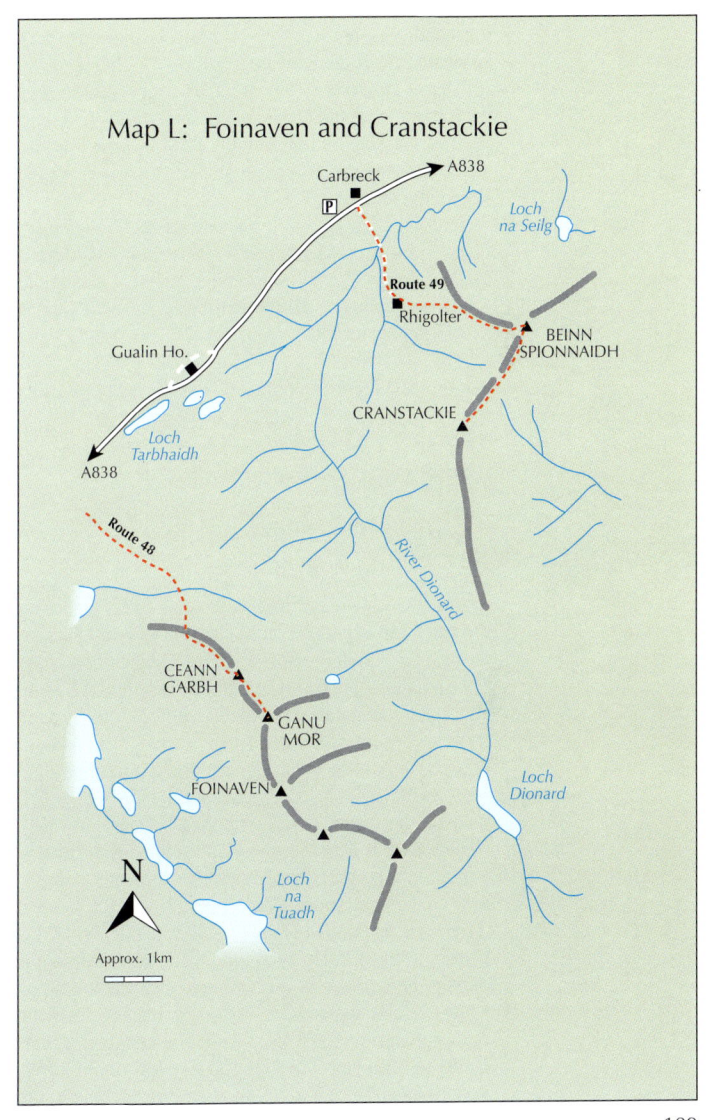

Map L: Foinaven and Cranstackie

tops, and most of them throw out spectacular side spurs eastward into Strath Dionard.

There are numerous possible routes of ascent, all of them interesting and challenging. Numerous ways could be devised from Strath Dionard, but I'll leave it to the adventurous reader to choose pioneering routes up this side of the range.

It is no exaggeration to say that if Foinaven were situated in the Lake District or Snowdonia it would have swarms of visitors every weekend, but here in the remote Reay Forest it enjoys a solitude which preserves its status as a mountain for the connoisseur.

Route 48: Ascent of Foinaven from the north-west

Distance:	13km
Height gain:	869ft
Map:	L
OS Map:	Landranger 9

Gualin House is virtually the only major landmark on the A838 between Rhiconich and the Kyle of Durness. However, it should be noted that the 1996 edition of the OS Landranger Sheet 9 (Cape Wrath) is now out of date. The start of the path into Strath Dionard is shown leaving the road by a bridge over a small tributary stream about 400m after passing the front door of the house (heading north-east). This is no longer the case.

The house (a private hunting lodge) has been bypassed on its north-west side and could now be passed without noticing it. The clues are its surround of trees, now on the right (south-east) of the road, and the fact that the bypass section is two-lane road while the rest of this stretch is single track. The path into Strath Dionard has been given a broad gravel surface to facilitate access by estate vehicles and now leaves the new road nearer to the house at an obvious kissing gate. The new path seems made for mountain bikes, but a large 'Bicycles prohibited' sign fixed to the new gate leaves no doubt as to the

ROUTE 48: ASCENT OF FOINAVEN FROM THE NORTH-WEST

landowner's opinion of that. Parking is available on the north-west side of the road 1km towards Durness.

Foinaven's northern top (Ceann Garbh) towers imposingly to the south from this viewpoint, and a bee-line route from here would take you straight to it, but a variation on this route is described below.

About 3km before Gualin House, approaching from the south (close to the point marked 143m on the OS map), there are a couple of parking spaces by the road. A south-easterly line from here, across boggy moorland, will bring you to the foot of an obvious break in the crags which encircle the north face of Ceann Garbh. The climb to the summit is steep and surprisingly long, but brings the summit underfoot without technical difficulty.

The sweeping ridges linking with Ganu Mor (914m) (the main top), and the top of A Ch'eir Ghorm (867m) are a joy to traverse. Narrow and graceful but without difficulty, they give a tremendous feeling of height and space. From the latter top, walk a few paces east to gain a view of the arrow-straight ridge of A Ch'eir Ghorm (see 'Alternatives' below).

Foinaven and Arkle

Continue along the main ridge, and a descent now leads to a prominent little peak (Lord Reay's Seat), below which is a steep step leading down to a narrow gap in the ridge called Cadha na Beucaich. This step can seem quite exposed as you approach it, but the steepest part is easily avoided by outflanking moves on the south-west side, and you are soon on the stiff climb to the final, unnamed summit at 806m.

Alternatives: For an alternative line of ascent, you could start from Gualin House, walking up Strath Dionard to the foot of A Ch'eir Ghorm (close to Loch Dionard) then ascending this airy ridge to the main ridge. This makes an excellent climb, and could also be used as an alternative descent, but be prepared for the extremely steep scree of the north-eastern end of the ridge.

A second alternative would be to reach the mountain from the south via Lone (see Route 45). This is a longer approach, but could be combined with an ascent of Arkle for a tough but memorable day. A variation on the return leg, if tackling both peaks, would be to make a descent from the Cadha na Beucaich gap to pick up a good path which skirts around the base of Arkle to emerge at Lochstack Lodge, just off the A838.

Cranstackie, 800m (2625ft), and Beinn Spionnaidh, 713m (2536ft)

Splendidly named, these two aloof mountains are the most northerly Corbetts, in fact the most northerly peaks of any consequence, on the British mainland. They are little visited and thus have a remote and lonely feel to them, which is an attraction to the true wilderness enthusiast, even though they are simple of shape and are completely overshadowed by their near neighbour Foinaven.

The views of the latter massif from the summit of Cranstackie are spectacular, and almost worth the ascent alone, while the northern panorama of coastline, with the Kyle of Durness and Loch Erribol, are almost as dramatic.

Route 49: Beinn Spionnaidh and Cranstackie from Carbreck

Distance:	11km
Height gain:	985m
Map:	L
OS Map:	Landranger 9

This route makes a good half-day outing, taking in the tops of both hills in a simple circuit with mostly easy (if wet) terrain underfoot.

Parking is available by the A838, near to the remote building of Carbreck (GR332592), and a stony dirt track leads from here to the farm buildings at Rhigolter. Passing in front of the farm house, a stile will be seen leading onto open fell, and from here it is then a simple matter of heading due east up steep, pathless terrain to gain the crest of the well-defined north-west ridge of Beinn Spionnaidh. The ridge climbs steadily up to emerge on the southern end of the slabby summit plateau, with the

Cranstackie and Rhigolter (photo: Andy Walmsley)

highest point a short way along the edge of the north-western escarpment.

Now head south-west, first over slabs and rocks, then over pleasant turf to reach the narrow col separating Spionnaidh from Cranstackie, which rears ahead impressively. The climb to the summit is quite easy, on mostly grassy terrain, and rocks make their presence felt only on the uppermost reaches. The summit plateau is a tilted waste of rocks and stones, with the cairn perched sensationally on the very edge of the steep northern slope. The views of Foinaven on a clear day are particularly impressive from here.

Returning to the col, descend easily into a broad corrie overlooking the A838. When the boggy floor of this hanging valley is reached, cross the stream and make a descending traverse northwards to reach Rhigolter and the track back to Carbreck.

Ben Hope, 927m (3040ft)

Ben Hope has but one claim to fame. It is Scotland's most northerly Munro, and apart from this distinction it is a completely unremarkable mountain. Simple of form, Ben Hope has none of the spectacular features of the flamboyant sandstone peaks further south, yet despite this it does have an imposing presence, standing alone in remote country, and its Munro status ensures it is one of the most climbed mountains in the north of Scotland. Had it been 50ft shorter it would surely have suffered worse obscurity than Canisp. However, although it cannot compare with Suilven – or even Stack Polly – for rocky ridges, Ben Hope does have a challenging north ridge, the section below the summit requiring good rock skills, especially in poor conditions. The southerly route described below is the usual route to the top.

Route 50: Ascent of Ben Hope from Strath More
The shortest route to the summit of Ben Hope starts from a large cattle shed by the roadside 3km south of the head

ROUTE 50: ASCENT OF BEN HOPE FROM STRATH MORE

Distance:	7km; 12km by alternative route
Height gain:	900m (both routes)
Map:	M
OS Map:	Landranger 9

of Loch Hope. A sign, roughly painted on a boulder, announces 'Ben Hope, way up', and the much trodden route is obvious, appearing as a wide swathe of black, muddy peat.

This initial pull up is steep and unpleasant due to the level of erosion, but the route improves once the crest of the Leitir Mhuiseil ridge (Ben Hope's south-west

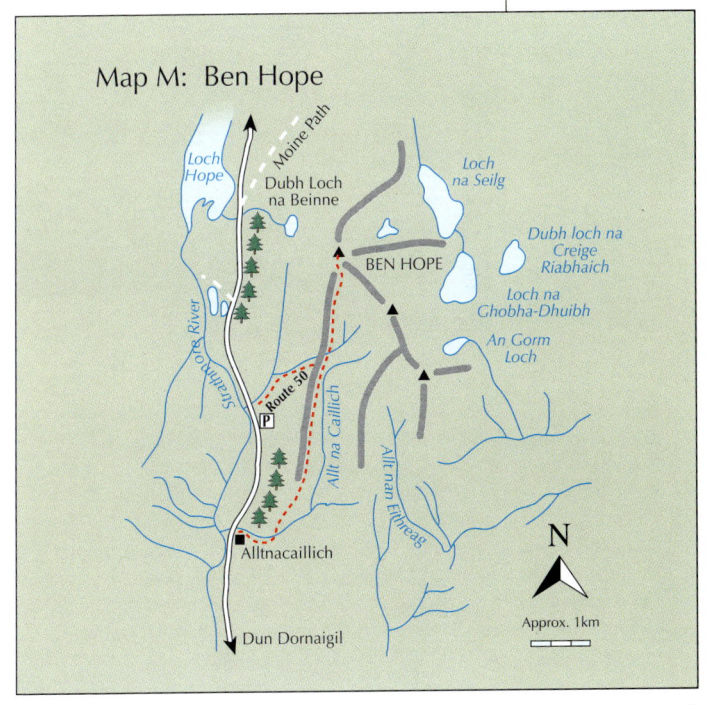

Map M: Ben Hope

The start of the direct route to Ben Hope (photo: Ian Roberts)

ridge) is reached. From here onwards the path is good and firm, climbing steadily up to the long summit plateau of the mountain.

Alternative: A longer but much pleasanter route starts further south, near the Dun Dornaigil broch ruins. This avoids the eroded initial climb described above and instead follows the Leitir Mhuiseil ridge throughout its length.

Limited parking is available on the roadsides near Alltnacaillich farm, and the path commences next to the farm house, climbing straight up to a waterfall (prominent on the skyline). The initial ascent is fairly steep, but the path is less eroded than the northern route and therefore more pleasant to climb. Once on the ridge and past the waterfall, it is a simple matter of following the escarpment (path) until the main 'tourist' route is joined.

THE EAST

As you move further away from the west coast in this part of Scotland the hills generally become less craggy, less shapely and often less interesting. However, there are exceptions to this rule, such as Ben Klibreck, Ben Loyal and the Morven group. These are all shapely and interesting hills and could not fairly be omitted from the book.

The eastern country has a lonely appeal of its own, and the seeker after solitude will perhaps find the empty spaces of the east the most appealing of all. Apart from the hills described in this book there are other possibilities in the area. The Ben Armine Forest is a huge area of wilderness criss-crossed with paths, and the Ben Griams are also worth a second look.

Most convenient bases for the east include Lairg, the east coast towns of Brora, Helmsdale and Dunbeath, as well as Altnaharra, Tongue and even Scourie, which has an easy cross-country link via the A838.

Ben Loyal, 764m (2506ft)

Ben Loyal is an object much admired and photographed by visitors to the far north. Its imposing appearance from the vicinity of Tongue, with its sweeping ridges and towering buttresses, makes it one of Scotland's most famous peaks, despite its relatively modest altitude.

However, although the traverse of all its tops makes a satisfying outing, it is probably fair to say that the ascent of Ben Loyal does not generally live up to the promise contained in its visual beauty.

Route 51: Ascent of Ben Loyal from Ribigill

Distance:	13km
Height gain:	762m
Map:	N
OS Map:	Landranger 10

The favoured starting point for the ascent of Ben Loyal is the large farm of Ribigill, but parking at the farm itself is

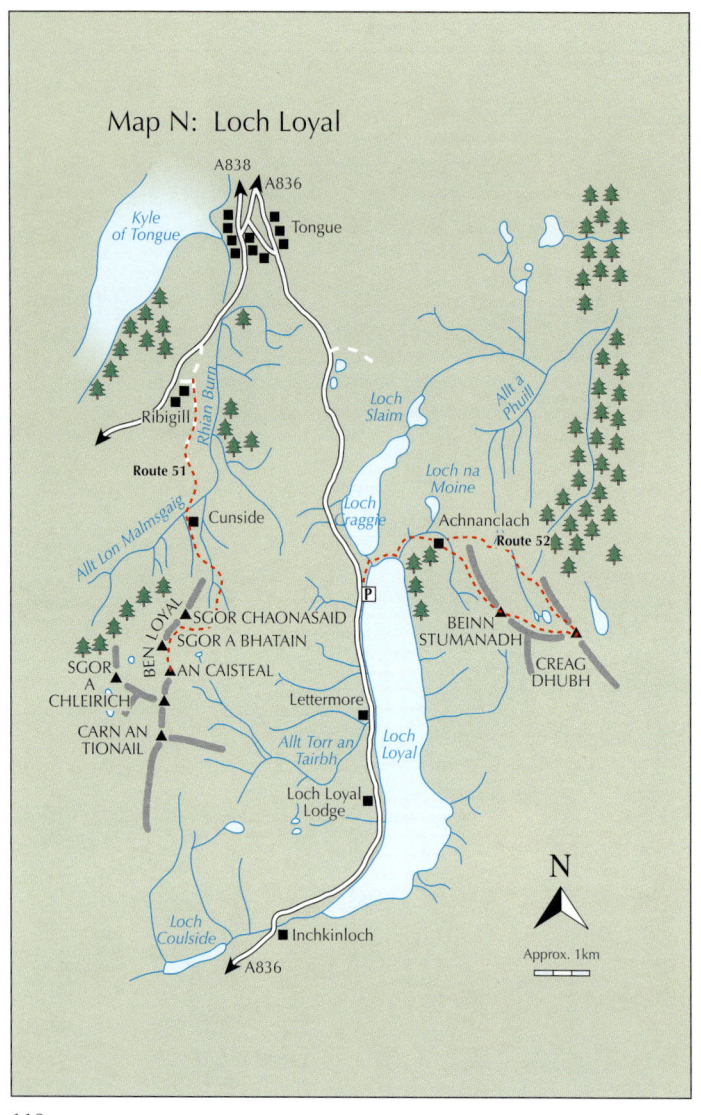

WALKING IN SCOTLAND'S FAR NORTH

Map N: Loch Loyal

Route 51: Ascent of Ben Loyal from Ribigill

discouraged. Instead, park by the cattle grid at the entrance to the farm lane (GR583546 – just after turning off the road south from Tongue).

The approach from Ribigill is initially along a well-used farm road, which can be very muddy and unpleasant in wet weather. This muddy lane becomes a stony Land Rover track and eventually a path as it approaches the vicinity of the derelict building at Cunside. Three streams have to be forded on this section, but the first two should give no trouble, unless the weather is very wet. However, the crossing of the third, the Allt Lon Malmsgaig near Cunside, is broad and usually at least calf-deep. It could prove troublesome after heavy rain.

Once safely across, the route heads straight up the hillside towards Sgor Chaonasaid, passing some 150m west of Cunside. As the slopes steepen the path veers left and winds its way pleasantly upward on mostly grassy or heathery terrain to eventually emerge onto the col between Sgor Chaonasaid and the minor top of Sgor a Bhatain. An Caisteal (the highest top) is seen to the

Ben Loyal

south, its rocky turreted summit easily overtopping the mainly grassy hummock of Sgor a Bhatain. The rocky turrets on the mountain's north-west face, below this latter top, which are a striking feature of Ben Loyal when seen from Tongue, are not at all evident from the summit ridge. In fact, the ridge hereabouts is quite mossy and broad, the summits having only limited outcrops of naked rock – a slight disappointment after admiring the hill's rugged appearance from afar.

If planning to traverse the southern tops, it is probably a good idea to head first for Sgor Chaonasaid. The scramble up to this northernmost summit, which is easiest on the right (east) side, gives sensational views over the Kyle of Tongue and goes some way towards making up for the mild terrain of the ridge.

Returning across the broad col to the south, an easy uphill walk leads to the summit rocks of An Caisteal at 764m. Ben Hope is well seen from here, and the sweeping ridges of the southern tops are suddenly revealed beyond a profound craggy drop.

Continuing southwards, after picking your way down this rocky declivity, a junction of ridges is reached at a minor top (741m on Landranger 10). Carn an Tionail is easily reached from here, and detours can also be

Alternative: If a much quieter approach to the mountain is desired, it is possible to start from the east, near Loch Loyal Lodge (GR618466). Parking is available at a number of places along Loch Loyal side, and although this side of the mountain is often dismissed as tedious, it actually lends itself better to a circular route.

Starting from the vicinity of Loch Loyal Lodge, a good route ascends steeply to Meall Eudainn and Cnoc nan Cuilean (557m) then descends to cross a boggy col by Loch na Beiste. Rough, steepening slopes are then climbed to reach Carn an Tionail, from where a traverse of An Caisteal will take you to the col, where the Ribigill route arrives on the ridge. From here, descend the path for 120m (400ft) then veer off due east to arrive on a broad 'shelf' containing Loch na Creige Riabhaich. The Allt Torr an Tairbh can be followed from here as it descends over rough slopes to a sizeable plateau at c.230m. Crossing this can be dreary, but it soon leads to the final descent back to the road at Lettermore, quite close to your starting point at Loch Loyal Lodge made out onto Sgor a Chleirich and the conical 568m top to the west of Loch Fionnaich. All these southern tops are quite remote from Ribigill, and the return to Cunside along the north-west edge of the Coille na Cuile woods is quite rough and trackless. If the weather is good, it is better to bag whichever tops take your fancy then return via the ridge to pick up your outward path for descent to Cunside – a more strenuous route, but one which gives a second opportunity to enjoy the views from the summit of An Caisteal.

Beinn Stumanadh, 527m (1729ft), and its Outliers

For those looking for even greater solitude than can be found on Cranstackie or Beinn Spionnaidh this small group of peaks on the east side of Loch Loyal will probably provide it. They make an ideal objective for a sunny bank holiday when most visitors to the area are heading for Ben Loyal and Ben Hope.

Beinn Stumanadh is the highest top of a ridge, running roughly west to east, which also includes Creag Dhubh and Meall an Spothaidh. This ridge throws down four spurs to the north, three of which provide a convenient route to the ridge. The easternmost of these, falling from the summit of Meall an Spothaidh, is less well defined and less convenient to approach.

The route described here follows the second most easterly spur in ascent, climbing to Creag Dhubh, traversing the ridge to Beinn Stumanadh in a convenient horseshoe then descending by either of the western spurs.

Route 52: Ascent of Beinn Stumanadh from Loch Loyal

At the north end of Loch Loyal, there is a convenient parking lay-by near an old ruin (spot height 119m on OS Landranger 10). From here, a path follows the loch shore, crossing a new footbridge over the short river linking Loch Craggie to Loch Loyal, and continues

Distance:	11km
Height gain:	472m
Map:	N
OS Map:	Landranger 10

around the northern shore of the loch, skirting the foot of Beinn Stumanadh's western spur (Sron Ruadh) to reach the open cottage of Achnanclach. From here, keep low and continue eastward, skirting a second spur to reach a gate in the deer fence, which gives access to the slopes of the third spur.

Climbing towards the crest of the spur, a second deer fence is reached, and it is probably better to climb this rather than make a long detour east to find a gate. This will demand a certain amount of agility as the fence is several metres high – care is required. Once on the crest, it is a simple matter to follow it over slabby rocks and short heather to the prominent summit cone of Creag Dhubh.

The ridge west from this summit gives easy walking – with great views to the north and south – over two subsidiary tops before descending slightly to a depression with a massive peat grough at the foot of Beinn Stumanadh. Steep climbing now follows on an indistinct path. Aim for an obvious heathery gully at the back of a shallow corrie which leads out onto the summit plateau and eventually to the trig point.

From here, either continue west to descend the western spur to Sron Ruadh (good views of Loch and Ben Loyal), or descend north via the second spur. Either of these descents will lead you quickly back to Achnanclach, from where outward steps can be retraced to the road at Loch Loyal head.

Ben Klibreck, 961m (3153ft)

Ben Klibreck, second most northerly Munro, is often dismissed as a bland grassy hill, but this does not to it justice.

BEN KLIBRECK

Map O: Ben Klibreck

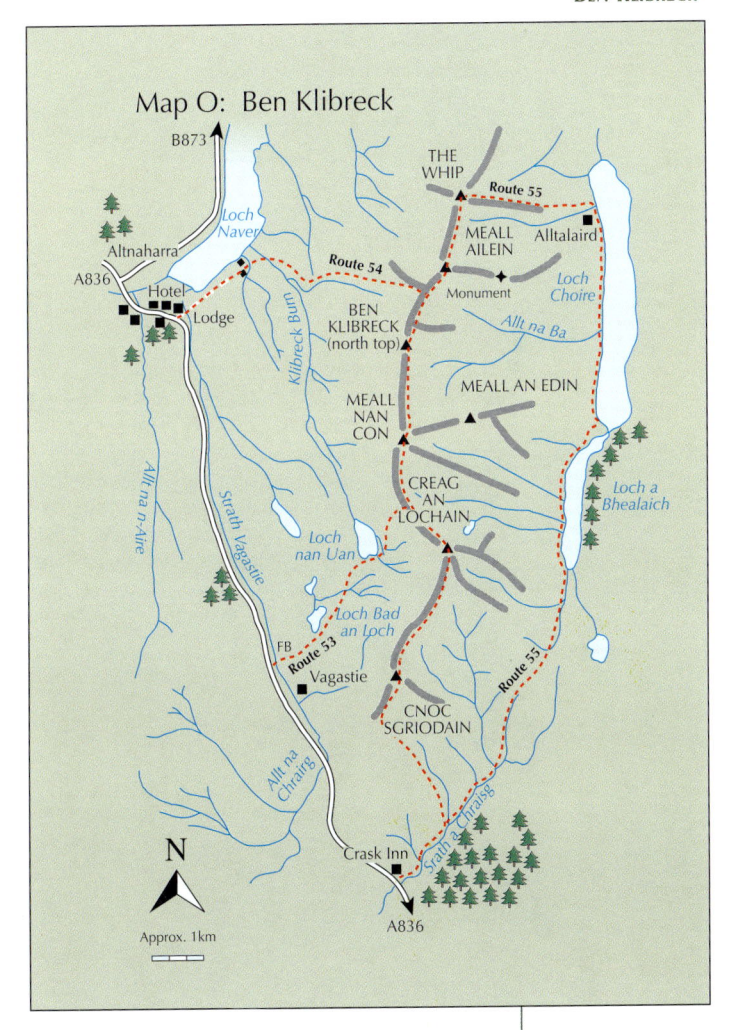

The broad ridges are indeed mostly grassy and much of the mountain has smooth rounded contours, but the shapely summit cone of Meall nan Con makes a superb

WALKING IN SCOTLAND'S FAR NORTH

mountain top, and the broad ridges provide a fine promenade high above the surrounding country.

Route 53: Ascent of Ben Klibreck (Meall nan Con) from Vagastie

Distance:	14km
Height gain:	792m
Map:	O
OS Map:	Landranger 16

This is the shortest ascent of Ben Klibreck. Park by the roadside near a footbridge over the river 800m north of the cottage at Vagastie (GR537289). From here, Meall nan Con is in view for almost the whole climb.

Leave the road on a boggy path, cross the footbridge and continue up wet grassy slopes, passing by a pretty little ravine to reach Loch Bad an Loch on a broad shelf containing a string of lochans. The path continues purposefully towards the peak, rising up slopes of grass

Ben Klibreck

and heather and finally petering out as the shore of Loch nan Uan is approached.

Above the lochan, the slope rears up steeply. The obvious objective is a shallow saddle on the ridge near the summit cone, but the direct line to here is excessively steep. To gain a slightly easier climb keep further right (south), climbing heathery slopes, followed by a shallow mossy gully, to a point where the angle begins to ease. At this point, watch out for a narrow trod contouring the slope and partially marked by a line of old broken wooden posts. Turn left along this to emerge on the col immediately below the final summit ridge. A small path continues up initially easy grass slopes, passing through a rocky band and finally climbing steeply up the the stony summit cone.

The summit itself is an excellent watchtower; small in extent and falling away steeply below, it gives a superb panorama. Ben Hope and Ben Loyal are prominent to the north, the Ben Armine and Loch Choire forests to the east. Loch Shin and the Fisherfield hills (with An Teallach) are in view to the south, and the peaks of Coigach, Assynt and Reay form the western skyline.

Route 54: Ascent of Ben Klibreck (Meall nan Con) from Altnaharra

Distance:	18km
Height gain:	1035m
Map:	O
OS Map:	Landranger 16

Altnaharra, an important local crossroads and prominently marked on road maps, is only a bleak scattering of cottages at the head of Loch Naver. However, it does have a post office, school and hotel, and could possibly be used as a base.

The ascent of Ben Klibreck from Altnaharra is possibly the least interesting of the routes offered here, but is also probably the easiest (though not the shortest – see Route

53). The beginning of the walk passes the stalker's cottage at Klibreck farm, and it is a good idea to ask permission to go on the mountain as stalking and culling activities are quite often undertaken there.

Continue from the farm, following a track across a stream and through a fence gate to reach the Klibreck Burn. The track continues, climbing easily at first and then steepening to finally zig-zag up onto the ridge near the top of Meall Ailein (GR610315). Good steady walking on an easy, broad ridge now leads to a gradual pull up onto the north-east end of the elongated summit ridge of Meall nan Con. The OS trig pillar, enclosed in a circular stone wind-shelter, is at the far end.

Route 55: The full traverse of Klibreck ridge from Crask Inn

Distance:	34km
Height gain:	1310m
Map:	O
OS Map:	Landranger 16

This is a superb expedition giving a real impression of the scale of Ben Klibreck and its outliers. It does require quite a long day though, unless you are tremendously fit. The full traverse of the Klibreck ridge makes an excellent winter walk, but a pre-dawn start would be required to complete the route in a short highland winter day. A bright day in March with snow on the high tops would be perfect, if you can arrange it!

Start from just south of the Crask Inn and follow a good path along Srath a Chraisg and over the narrow defile of Bealach Easach to reach Loch a Bhealaich. The path continues to the shore of the much larger Loch Choire, where it meets another path emerging from the fastnesses of the Ben Armine deer forest.

Follow this path north-eastwards along the shore of the loch, with the bulk of Ben Klibreck towering to your left, to reach a Land Rover track at the far end, opposite

Loch Choire lodge. From here, head north-west up long easy slopes to arrive at the summit of The Whip (GR625321), the most northerly of Klibreck's high tops. Now head south-west across a broad saddle and climb a stiff slope to Meall Ailein and the main ridge.

The walking is now along a superb high-level promenade – well defined and graceful, with easy terrain underfoot. Progress along here is fast and easy, and the slim summit ridge of Meall nan Con is soon gained.

Descend from the top due west to pick up a path which threads through a short area of rocky ground then curves southwards on excellent short turf again. The 807m summit of Creag an Lochan can be contoured on a well-marked stalkers' path on the west side, but the traverse of this minor top is easy and well worthwhile for its excellent views of the Loch Choire glen below. The best views are obtained by keeping close to the scarp edge above Loch an Fhuarain, but once the highest point has been passed curve westward to descend easy grass slopes on a rapidly broadening ridge towards Cnoc Sgriodain – the last top of the day.

The slopes between here and Crask can be descended almost anywhere, but the lower part is comprised of a rough and boggy heather moor. My advice is to head south, initially on a dry grassy spur then over rough heather to pick up the path in Srath a Chraisg for a relatively easy walk back to the inn.

Morven, 706m (2316ft), and Scaraben, 626m (2053ft)

Although quite remote from the main areas of interest in the far north, these two peaks are worth an expedition. They are located in a wild and unfrequented area, and are abrupt and shapely hills which could stand shoulder to shoulder with the Assynt peaks without disgrace. Morven, particularly, is a fine conical object which demands to be climbed, and its smaller neighbour, Maiden Pap (484m), is almost a miniature replica. Both

WALKING IN SCOTLAND'S FAR NORTH

give excellent views of the desolate country between Strath of Kildonan and the east coast. Scaraben is less imposing than its neighbours, but fits well into a circular walk in the area.

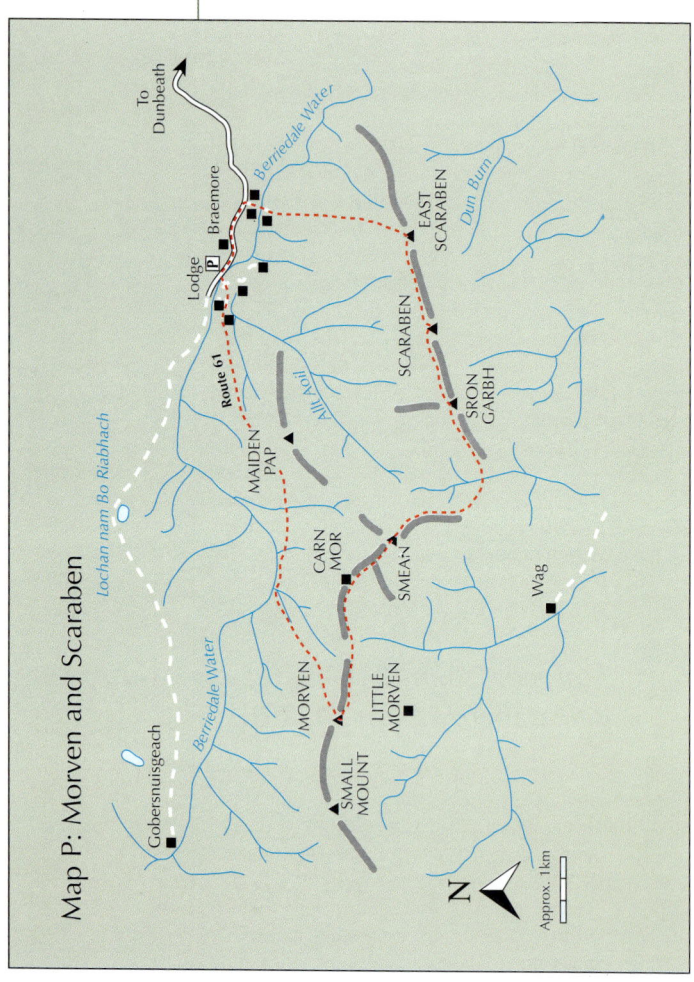

Map P: Morven and Scaraben

ROUTE 56: ASCENT OF MORVEN FROM BRAEMORE

Travelling north on the A9, just before reaching Dunbeath, a branch road leads off for some 8km (5 miles) to Braemore Lodge. By the bridge over the Berriedale Water, there is a phone box and a parking space big enough for two cars (usually empty). This is the best starting point for the ascent of Morven.

Route 56: Ascent of Morven from Braemore

Distance:	22km
Height gain:	1280m
Map:	P
OS Map:	Landranger 17

A gravelled Land Rover track continues from the bridge over the Berriedale Water to wind between the farm buildings of Braeval. A sign on the last cottage requests walkers to inform the keeper of their route, but the cottage is sometimes empty, leaving walkers with the dilemma of whether to continue. I'll leave it up to you to

The sandstone cone of Morven (photo: Andy Walmsley)

129

decide, if this is the case. The gravelled track continues purposefully up through a small plantation (not marked on OS Sheet 17) with Maiden Pap directly ahead. After crossing a wide and shallow saddle, the track descends to the bothy at Corrichoich, where it ends.

From this point onward, paths are at best sketchy. Continue initially along the south bank of the stream, passing the site of an old wheelhouse, marked on the map but very indistinct on the ground, to a junction with a sizeable tributary. A thin path leads up the north-west (true left) bank of this stream, but peters out in heathery terrain as the foot of Morven's final pyramid approaches.

Looking at the peak from here, the best route lies up the right skyline. Traverse across (virtually due west) to the foot of the summit cone and prepare for some serious hard labour. The summit is over 350m above at this point and the route to it is very steep and unrelenting, climbing over pathless slopes of heather and bilberry with a jumble of rocks beneath.

After gaining the Morven summit and regaining your breath, you can survey your ascent route and the possible alternatives for return. Obviously, the quickest alternative is to retrace your outward steps, but if a longer expedition is required descend the eastern slope (just as steep as your ascent route) then follow the rough and indistinct ridge as it traverses eastwards over Carn Mor, Smean and Scaraben to East Scaraben. From the summit of this last top, a descent can be made over typically rough terrain to a bridge over the Berriedale Water at GR083297, from where it is a simple stroll back along the road to your parked vehicle.

Alternative: On the ridge towards Scaraben, if it is required to visit Maiden Pap, an out-and-back detour across a marshy depression from the summit of Smean is a possibility. It would also be possible to shorten the expedition by descending from Maiden Pap back to Braeval. If intending to do this, leave the top of Maiden Pap in a westerly direction to avoid its northern crags, then head north to reach the Corrichoich track at its high point. This makes an interesting half-day outing.

LONGER MOUNTAIN TRAVERSES

Route 57: The Assynt Horseshoe

Distance:	56km
Height gain:	3350m (excluding Suilven)
OS Map:	Landranger 15

The Assynt Horseshoe is an arduous outing for serious ultra-distance types only. To complete the circuit in one day is really the preserve of hill runners or the strongest of mountain walkers, and even for these it will probably demand at least 12 hours of effort. However, lesser mortals can still enjoy the round as a two-day challenge with a convenient wild camp or bivouac en-route, and this approach will probably give a more enjoyable experience, especially if you are lucky with the weather.

The best starting point for the horseshoe is Little Assynt. There is an unavoidable 3.2km (2 miles) of road by Loch Assynt, and going clockwise from here gets it out of the way at the start. Parking is available by the roadside 200m east of the Little Assynt buildings (see Route 16), and the A837 can be followed north-east from here to the cottage of Tumore, where the ascent of Quinag begins. Refer to Route 30 for more details of the climb to the Bealach a Chornaidh.

Once on the bealach you can decide whether to visit Quinag's main summit (or all its summits!) or to simply turn right and head up to Spidean Coinich. Whichever tops you decide to visit, you will eventually arrive on the top of Spidean (which is Quinag's southernmost top) and then descend the stony south-east ridge to reach the A894 by a large parking area (see start point of Route 28).

The next objective is Glas Bheinn, which rises ahead as a huge whaleback waste of grey scree. It is quite possible to just climb directly up to the summit on a bearing from here, but a far more comfortable alternative is to cross initial heathery slopes in an easterly direction to pick up a good path heading north from Ardvreck Castle to Loch na Gainmhich. Follow this path to its highest point, then strike up the slopes of Glas Bheinn using a steep but grassy streak (too shallow to be called a gully) to reach the north end of the ridge and a fairly pleasant walk to the summit.

From the bouldery chaos of Glas Bheinn's top, head south-east to reach the edge of the eastern escarpment, which can then be followed to pick up a path leading down to a shallow col (cairns) between Glas Bheinn and Beinn Uidhe. This is the col which is crossed en route from Inchnadamph to the Eas a Chual Aluinn waterfall (see Route 26). From here the ridge is a mass of stones. No path can survive in this terrain, and it is simply a matter of keeping to the high ground until the top of Beinn Uidhe is reached.

Assuming visibility is good, Beinn an Fhurain and Na Tuadhan (spot height 860m on OS Landranger 15) can be seen to the south, with Conival looming behind them, but the route across the intervening ground can be confusing, especially if visibility is poor. The first aim is to reach the pleasant shores of Loch nan Cuaran, but instead of descending to the north-western end of the loch (hideous boulder scree), keep to the crest of the ridge, passing to the north-east of it. Easier slopes can then be descended to reach the loch's eastern end.

A pleasant grassy oasis now gives a respite from rocks and boulders. Follow the green sward southward, but after 800–1000m veer to the east to gain a scarp edge overlooking the valley of the Garbh Allt and an increasingly well-defined ridge leading to the summit of Na Tuadhan. Although Beinn an Fhurain is named on the OS map further west, the marked summit is actually a worthless hump interrupting the slopes decending from the much higher Na Tuadhan. If this mountain massif is called Beinn an Fhurain, then Na Tuadhan is the true summit and is not only the highest point but also the most obvious objective, its craggy top poised on the edge of tremendous crags plunging down to Coire a Mhadaidh and Garbh Allt.

Another tricky bit of route-finding now follows. A tiny lochan is shown on the map and this seems to be on

ROUTE 57: THE ASSYNT HORSESHOE

an obvious line to Conival, avoiding the crags immediately below the summit, but a direct descent to this lochan is extremely unpleasant on account of a fiendishly loose slope of boulders. Instead, return across the summit plateau in an easterly direction for 300m before gently curving round to the south, passing the lochan on your left and enjoying some grassy terrain on the approach to Conival. At the bealach, the main path from Inchnadamph via Traligill is met, and the way up Conival's north ridge to the summit is then obvious.

The summit of Ben More Assynt is a rough and rocky 30 minutes away. It doesn't lie on the logical horseshoe ridge route, but does merit a visit if time allows. It is the 'big mountain of Assynt' after all. The next summit on the horseshoe is Breabag, but huge crags falling from Conival's summit bar a direct line from here. The best way to gain access to it is by descending a wide scree slope which drops into Garbh Coire from the Conival/Ben More ridge (see Route 25) then skirting around the foot of the crags into a narrow trough at the head of Gleann Dubh (Traligill valley). Breabag Tarsuinn (the most northerly top) is then easily reached.

Suilven from Canisp (photo: Andy Walmsley)

The terrain continues stony across the wide expanses of Breabag, but after traversing the second summit the ridge descends to a broad and slightly grassier saddle with a little lochan on its western side. This is the head of the Alt nan Uamh valley and is the start of the descent to the A837. However, the main summit lies further south and an out-and-back detour is required to reach it (see Route 25). Alternatively, you could descend directly from the main summit to reach the Allt nan Uamh near the 'bone caves', but this is a rougher route.

Assuming you have opted for the out-and-back detour and have returned from the main top, follow the little stream which issues from the lochan. After crossing a marshy hollow the valley narrows, and the stream then tumbles over a succession of charming little waterfalls and cascades. For those on a two-day trip, this would be a good place for your overnight camp/bivvy.

Continuing down, take a gradually higher line as the stream heads for a narrow ravine, thus avoiding an awkward narrowing of the valley above a (usually dry) waterfall (see Route 22). This is now limestone country, and the stream disappears underground for a while, re-emerging suddenly at a prominent spring further downstream. High on the left (south) side of the valley the 'bone caves', where prehistoric remains have been found, can be seen, and from here a good path leads you down to the A837 road at the Allt nan Uamh parking place (GR253179).

Canisp is now the obvious next climb, but a beeline from here is not recommended. Although that would be the shortest way, it is easier to walk S along the road to the start of Route 19 and make the ascent from there. It is possible to follow the River Loanan upstream from Allt nan Uamh and join Route 19 at the outflow from Loch Awe, but this is a rougher route and will cost you time. The choice is yours.

Canisp is the last of the logical peaks on the Assynt Horseshoe, but few will stand on its summit and not be tempted to make a detour to Suilven, which looks magnificent across the glen. A lot will depend on your level of fitness, commitment or enthusiasm, as well as the amount of

ROUTE 58: A REAY TRAVERSE

time you have left for the return to Little Assynt, but the detour is not to be embarked upon lightly. Suilven is a tough climb whichever way you approach it, and the walk out from Glen Canisp can seem endless at the end of a route like this.

Descend Canisp's splendid north-west ridge to reach a good path traversing the Glencanisp Forest from Elphin to Lochinver and follow this westward towards the latter place. After crossing to the south side of the river on a good footbridge the path passes a cairn on the left, marking the start of the path up Suilven (Route 14/17), then descends to cross another footbridge back onto the north side.

Shortly, you arrive at a walled enclosure below the estate bothy of Suileag, and at the far end of the wall turn right on another good path to the bothy. A small path will be seen climbing up a rough slope west of the building (cairned), and this leads over a boggy spur to a lonely string of lochans (Loch Bad an t-Sluic, Loch Crom and Loch an Leothaid). After threading between these, the path makes a stiff pull up to a boggy col between Cnoc an Leothaid and An Leathad (a testing little climb at this stage of the walk).

A descent through a little stream gully and a short indistinct section bring you to the ford across the Allt an Tiaghaich, which could be troublesome in wet weather, and then to Little Assynt and the end of the circuit. For more detail of the route from Glencanisp to Little Assynt see Route 16.

Route 58: A Reay traverse

Distance:	40km (less 7km if excluding Arkle)
Height gain:	3020m (less 580m if excluding Arkle)
Map:	J
OS Map:	Landranger 9, 15, 16

This is a tough route through a wild area of lonely mountains. It is advisable to choose a period of settled weather to attempt the route or, alternatively, to be 100% confident in your experience, fitness and navigational ability if the weather is a bit unsettled. Being an end-to-end journey rather than a circuit, transport will be needed at each end, and the usual plan of dropping a car at the far end then returning to the start in a second vehicle will be the most convenient solution. For those with only one vehicle available, it may be possible to park at the north-west end of the route and get a post bus from Gualin House to Merkland. Check with Royal Mail as to current routes and timetables.

Most people will need a bivouac or wild camp on a route this long, and the recommended location for this is the area below Creagan Meall Horn (GR335453), where there are good sheltered hollows, running water and pleasant little tarns.

Start from the cottage at West Merkland as if heading for Ben Hee (Route 37), but continue up the Land Rover track for a further kilometre to about GR396352, where the Allt na Glaise is crossed.

Now climb straight up an increasingly shapely ridge to the top of Carn an Tionail. Looking west from here, a

The summit ridge of Arkle (photo: Andy Walmsley)

ROUTE 58: A REAY TRAVERSE

daunting gulf containing Lochan a Bhealaich separates you from Carn Dearg, eastern outlier of the Meallan Liath massif. Cross this gulf (which is not as bad as it looks) and continue west from Carn Dearg along the main ridge, with great views down into the northern corries. This ridge leads to the obvious top of Meallan Liath Coire Mhic Dhughaill (801m), the obviously highest summit hereabouts.

From Meallan Liath head north, passing over the top of Meall Garbh, and descend to the lonely pass of Bealach na Feithe, which separates the Meallan Liath group from the Sabhals and Meall Horn.

Continue straight ahead, climbing a steep and rough slope to Sabhal Beag, and then follow the ridge as it descends, curving north-west to a broad saddle under Sabhal More. A stiff pull brings you to the top of this latter summit, then an easy ridge gives good walking over the top of Meall Horn (cairn) to Creagan Meall Horn. All these hills have bald and rather featureless summits.

Crags bar a direct continuation from Creagan Meall Horn, and a slight back-track is required to reach easier ground on the south side of the hill, where a descent to the head of the Allt Horn can be made (bivouac/camp sites nearby). Foinaven could be climbed direct from here, via a long and featureless slope to the southernmost summit (and this is a possible short-cut), but the recommended route heads west to ascend roughly above a splendid rim of crags to Meall Aonghais and thence to Arkle.

After traversing Arkle's excellent summit ridge (easy but exhilarating) the continuation from the main summit to Foinaven is blocked by an extremely steep and rough slope to the north-east. To circumvent this, descend instead to the north-west (Sail Mor). The slope is still steep and rough, but it is preferable to the north-eastern one, and it leads down to a distinct path coming around the foot of the mountain from Lochstack Lodge. Turn right along this path and follow it past Loch na Tuadh until it begins climbing up the facing slopes of the Foinaven ridge. A thin track veers leftwards here, but don't worry too much if it is missed; the next stage is simply a matter of climbing arduously up the rough scree below Cadha na Beucaich (roughly north-east).

Once on the col, the facing prow of Lord Reay's Seat to the north looks truly formidable, but it is turned easily on the left (scree) and the ridge is then obvious, sweeping gracefully over two lower summits to Ganu Mor (914m), the highest top and virtually a Munro.

A number of ways are possible from here, all of them steep, rough and arduous. My recommendation is to continue north to the last top (Ceann Garbh) and descend from there. The initial descent north-west of the top is steep but easy, but bands of crag lower down force you to head further west to avoid them. Once below the craggy ground, resume your north-westerly line across a wet and heathery moor to emerge on the road 2km south-west of Gualin House.

Route 59: A long ascent of Cranstackie

Distance:	34km
Height gain:	2100m
Map:	Q
OS Map:	Landranger 9

Cranstackie and Beinn Spionnaidh are the highest tops on a long ridge separating the River Dionard/Kyle of Durness from Loch Eriboll. After descending from Beinn Spionnaidh quite grassily, the ridge makes a final rocky upsurge at the summit Bienn Ceannabeinne (383m) before plunging to sea level at Traigh na h-Uamhag, where there is possibly the best sandy cove on the north coast. The traverse of this ridge in both directions, starting from the north coast, makes an excellent, but demanding, mountain day with the possibility of a superb sea-swim if the day is favourable (admittedly rare, but not unheard of).

Near the isolated building of Ceannabienne (pronounced 'ken-a ben') there is a large parking lay-by overlooking the beach. Start from here and climb easy

ROUTE 59: A LONG ASCENT OF CRANSTACKIE

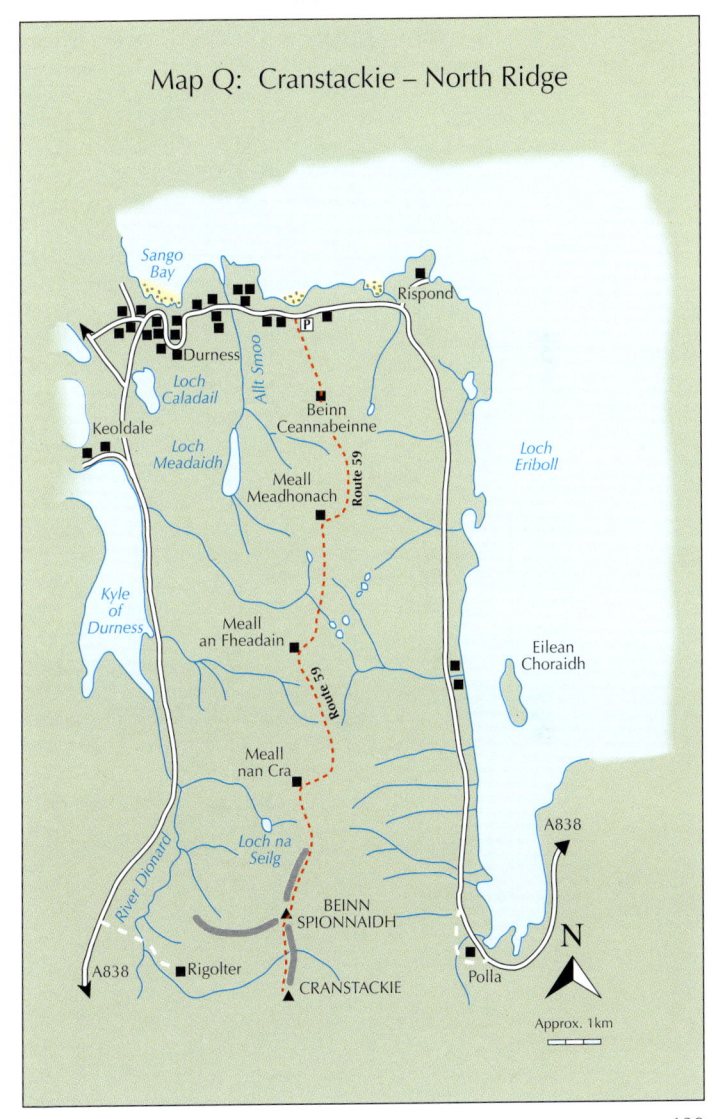

Map Q: Cranstackie – North Ridge

grass slopes with a few rock outcrops to the top of Bienn Ceannabeinne, on the edge of a rocky escarpment. Continue south from here (avoiding craggy ground) to reach a col with a good path leading off towards Durness. Now swing west and climb up to the undistinguished summit of Meall Meadhonach (422m).

Take a south-westerly line from the summit, following the ill-defined line of the ridge (difficult in mist) to another small col and then to the top of Meall an Fheadain (334m). The summits along this part of the ridge are uninspiring, but this is all good wild country, and the much sterner bulk of Beinn Spionnaidh looms ahead.

The next section of ridge is also rather ill-defined; the best line heads initially south then curves west to avoid the in-cut hollow of Bealach Mor and climbs grassy slopes to Meall nan Cra (490m). Now the moor becomes a ridge.

Descend to a wide col and climb the rocky prow of Carn an Righ, at the end of Beinn Spionnaid's summit ridge. The ascent is steep and moderately rough, but comes out onto an excellent tilted scarp edge which leads all the way to the summit of the mountain at 773m.

To reach Cranstackie, head down easy-angled slopes – initially stony but becoming grassy – to the narrow trough which separates the two mountains. The climb to the summit goes initially up a nice ridge then over a final boulder slope to the cairn, which is perched on the very edge of the steep western slope. It is a fine culmination of this long climb.

INTERESTING LOW-LEVEL WALKS

Route 60: Eas a Chual Aluinn

Distance:	10km
Height gain:	396m
OS Map:	Landranger 15

This spectacular waterfall, the highest in Britain, can be reached most easily from the shore of Loch na Gainmhich by the A894 road 5km (3 miles) south of Kylesku (GR240290). Parking is available by the roadside and the path commences along the north side of the loch, passing above an 18m (60ft) waterfall which is unnamed but well worth seeing. Take care on the peaty edge overlooking the fall (not very secure). This fall can also be viewed from below (see Route 26).

The path crosses rutted, boggy ground, then becomes stony and climbs steadily towards the Bealach a Bhuirich. Just before the highest point of the path, the sizeable Lochan Bealach a Bhuirich is passed on the

The Eas a Chual Aluinn – Britain's highest waterfall

right amid slabs of grey gneiss – ideal for sunbathing in exceptional weather.

Beyond the pass, the path descends to cross the Eas a Chual Aluinn stream, then continues in the direction of the Glas Bheinn/Beinn Uidhe divide. At the stream crossing, leave the main track and follow one of two peaty paths following the stream on either bank. The southernmost of these is best, and it leads to the edge of the fall. Take extreme care hereabouts, as the escarpment breaks away in a series of loose peaty ledges. The best view of the Eas a Chual Aluinn's spectacular 650ft plunge is obtained by heading south along the top edge of the cliff to a point where the angle eases and a descent can be made onto broader, safer terraces in full view of the fall.

The recommended return is via the outward route. Don't be lured into attempting a walk-out along the shore of Lochs Beag and Glencoul; there is no path and the terrain is very rough, involving a hair-raising traverse on a steep grass slope above cliffs at one point.

Route 61: The Culnacraig coastal path

Distance:	9km (one way)
Height gain:	215m (one way)
OS Map:	Landranger 15

This spectacularly scenic path links Ardmair with Culnacraig and Achiltibuie, snaking its way along the lower part of Ben Mor Coigach's south-western crags. It makes an ideal link in a circular traverse of Ben Mor's summit ridge, but also makes a very pleasant two-way walk, especially useful on a day when the tops are in cloud.

Start from the parking area at GR135015 (marked on the OS map), the approach to which involves threading your vehicle between the buildings of Blughasary, which display multiple 'No parking' signs. Beyond the buildings, a gate gives access to a largish parking place at a respectable distance from the house.

Route 62: To Sandwood Bay and Cape Wrath

Cross a footbridge over the River Runie, running in an interesting rocky channel here, and turn left along a path towards the ancient fort of Dun Canna and the sea shore. After 2km (1¼ miles) a gate on the right gives access to a very steep slope, up which the Culnacraig path scrambles with difficulty. Signs attached to boulders on the initial slope give warnings about the dangers of the path, but in reasonable conditions it is quite straight forward.

As height is gained, the path heads across broad terraces above the sea, with superb views over Isle Martin and Ardmair Bay. After undulating for a while across a couple of gentle spurs, the path makes a big descent back to sea level before climbing again to skirt low sea cliffs to Culnacraig.

Achiltibuie is just up the coast from here, and the Acheninver Youth Hostel is also nearby.

Route 62: To Sandwood Bay and Cape Wrath

Distance:	14km
Height gain:	200m
OS Map:	Landranger 9

The beautifully wild beach at Sandwood Bay has been spared the horrors of development, people, litter and ugly static caravans by its location 6.4km (4miles) from the nearest road. The quality of this beach is on a par with that at Oldshoremore, but its more secluded location lends it an appeal and an aura which is possibly unequalled by any other beach in Britain.

However, the erosion of the existing path is evidence of its growing popularity, and the amenable nature of the terrain would make the building of a road very easy. At present, the Sandwood estate is determined to keep vehicles out (including mountain bikes), so the tranquillity of the beach is safe for the moment.

The path begins from Blairmore (GR195600), where there is a large parking place. Commencing as a broad unsurfaced vehicle track, the path meanders easily through

Am Buachaille and Sandwood Bay

bland moorland to Loch na Gainimh, where another track joins from the right. Keep left here, skirting the east end of the loch to climb gently over a very easy col and descend to a small pool. The track now deteriorates rapidly, descending to Loch a Mhuilinn, where it ends and an eroded path continues around the loch and up to a further col (also extremely easy) overlooking the beach. An easy descent, initially grassy, leads down to a large area of dunes and marram at the back of Sandwood Bay.

On a stormy day, the bay can be quite magnificently wild, with a spume-laden turquoise sea pounding the shore. On a calm and sunny day, the sea is very tempting for swimming, but despite its remoteness there are few days during summer when the beach is without visitors, so make sure you pack a costume!

It is possible to continue along the coast to Cape Wrath, but the route is altogether more arduous than the path to Sandwood Bay. There are a number of considerable descents and re-ascents necessary to cross sea inlets, and the terrain is rough, pathless moorland. Additionally, the only convenient return is back over the same ground. Add 26km and 700m of extra climbing for

ROUTE 62: TO SANDWOOD BAY AND CAPE WRATH

the two-way trip from Sandwood to the Cape and back. Definitely one for strong walkers only.

Another possible excursion from the bay is along the southern edge to the sea stack of Am Buachaille, clearly visible from the beach. Climbing up from the sands, a small path will be seen leading off from a grassy neck to traverse across the top of low cliffs to a point opposite the stack. Am Buachaille was first climbed by Tom Patey and John Cleare in the 1960s. They used a ladder to cross the narrow channel below the stack, but were almost cut off by the tide when returning after the climb.

If you have an appetite for some rougher walking, you can continue from Am Buachaille along the coast to arrive back at Blairmore via Sheigra. This is a slightly longer and rougher route than the direct path, but much more scenic.

Other Routes

The above routes are by no means the only worthwhile low-level routes in the far north. In fact, a perusal of any of the OS Landranger sheets will reveal a network of ancient paths winding their way between the mountains. These paths are sometimes indistinct on the ground and are always wet underfoot, but often cover large distances through some of the loneliest country available in Britain.

The Ben Armine Forest to the south-east of Ben Klibreck on Landranger 16 is an example. A network of paths criss-cross this area and seems to offer a huge opportunity for wilderness walks. The area is a prime example of the possibilities open to the adventurous explorer in the far north. Happy travelling!

APPENDIX A:
Sources of Information

Durness Tourist Information Centre
Durine
Durness
By Lairg
Sutherland IV27 4PN
Tel: 01971 511259
Fax: 01971 511368
E-mail: durness@host.co.uk

Lochinver Tourist Information Centre
Assynt Visitor Centre
Main Street
Lochinver
By Lairg
Sutherland IV27 4LX
Tel: 01571 844330
Fax: 01571 844373
E-mail: lochinver@host.co.uk

Ullapool Tourist Information Centre
Argyle Street
Ullapool
Ross-shire IV26 2UB
Tel: 01854 612135
Fax: 01854 613031
Email: Ullapool@host.co.uk

**North Kessock
Tourist Information Centre**
Picnic Site
North Kessock
Ross-shire
(Just north of Kessock Bridge,
Inverness)
IV1 1XB
Tel: 01463 731505
Fax: 01463 731701
E-mail: nkessock@host.co.uk

Inverness Tourist Information Centre
(Highlands of Scotland Tourist Board)
Castle Wynd
Inverness
Scotland
IV2 3BJ
Tel: 01463 234353
Fax: 01463 710609
E-mail: inverness@host.co.uk

**Highlands of Scotland
Tourist Board website:**
www.host.co.uk

Other useful websites:

www.assynt.co.uk
– website of the Assynt Tourism Group

www.scotland-index.co.uk
– massive amounts of information on all areas of Scotland.

www.scotland-info.co.uk
– the internet guide to Scotland

www.itv-weather.co.uk
– an excellent interactive weather guide with five-day forecasts for many locations in the far north.

APPENDIX B:
The Peaks (by height)

Mountain	metres	feet	page
Ben More Assynt	998	3274	67
Conival	984	3228	67
Ben Klibreck	961	3153	122
Ben Hope	927	3041	114
Foinaven	914	2999	108
Ben Hee	873	2864	95
Na Tuadhan	860	2821	76
Cul Mor	849	2785	50
Canisp	846	2776	62
Quinag	808	2651	77
Meallan Liath Coire Mhic Dhughaill	801	2628	98
Breabag	800	2625	65
Cranstackie	800	2625	112
Beinn Leoid	792	2598	85
Arkle	787	2582	105
Meall Horn	777	2549	102
Glas Bheinn	776	2546	73
Cul Beag	769	2523	43
Spidean Coinnich	764	2507	77
Ben Loyal	764	2507	117
Meallan a Chuail	750	2461	85
Ben More Coigach	743	2438	37
Beinn Uidhe	740	2428	73
Suilven	731	2398	55
Sabhal Beag	729	2392	102
Ben Stack	721	2365	91
Breabag North	715	2346	67
Beinn Spionnaidh	713	2339	112
Morven	706	2316	127
Sabhal Mor	703	2306	102
Scaraben	626	2054	127
Breabag Tarsuinn	625	2051	67
Stac Pollaidh	613	2011	46
Ben Stumanadh	527	1729	121

APPENDIX C:
The Peaks (alphabetically)

Mountain	metres	feet	page
Arkle	787	2582	105
Beinn Leoid	792	2598	85
Beinn Spionnaidh	713	2339	112
Beinn Uidhe	740	2428	73
Ben Hee	873	2864	95
Ben Hope	927	3041	114
Ben Klibreck	961	3153	122
Ben Loyal	764	2507	117
Ben More Assynt	998	3274	67
Ben More Coigach	743	2438	37
Ben Stack	721	2365	91
Ben Stumanadh	527	1729	121
Breabag	800	2625	65
Breabag North	715	2346	67
Breabag Tarsuinn	625	2051	67
Canisp	846	2776	62
Conival	984	3228	67
Cranstackie	800	2625	112
Cul Beag	769	2523	43
Cul Mor	849	2785	50
Foinaven	914	2999	108
Glas Bheinn	776	2546	73
Meall Horn	777	2549	102
Meallan a Chuail	750	2461	85
Meallan Liath Coire Mhic Dhughaill	801	2628	98
Morven	706	2316	127
Na Tuadhan	860	2821	76
Quinag	808	2651	77
Sabhal Beag	729	2392	102
Sabhal Mor	703	2306	102
Scaraben	626	2054	127
Spidean Coinnich	764	2507	77
Stac Pollaidh	613	2011	46
Suilven	731	2398	55

APPENDIX D:
List of Walking Routes

	Route	km	m/ascent	page
1	Ben More Coigach: Ascent from Acheninver Youth Hostel	16.0	914	37
2	Ben More Coigach: Ascent from the Achiltibuie road	15.0	914	40
3	Cul Beag: Ascent from Drumrunie	3.1	670	43
4	Cul Beag: Ascent from Linneraineach	6.5	701	44
5	Cul Beag: Link route to Stac Pollaidh	5.0	442	45
6	Stac Pollaidh: Ascent to the main col from Loch Lurgain	3.2	550	46
7	Stac Pollaidh: Summit ridge traverse	variable	variable	48
8	Cul Mor: Ascent from Knockanrock	10.0	732	50
9	Cul Mor: Ascent from the A835 via An Laogh	13.0	792	51
10	Cul Mor: Ascent from Linneraineach via SW face	13.0	975	52
11	Cul Mor: Link route to Cul Beag	4.0	700	53
12	Suilven: Approach from Elphin	22.0	396	55
13	Suilven: Approach from Lochinver	19.0	244	56
14	Suilven: Ascent from the north-east	6.5	580	57
15	Suilven: Ascent from Inverkirkaig	22.0	762	57
16	Suilven: Approach from Little Assynt	16.0	457	60
17	Suilven: Summit ridge traverse	variable	variable	61
18	Canisp: Ascent from Little Assynt	26.0	1158	62
19	Canisp: Ascent from Loch Awe	12.0	700	62
20	Canisp: Link route to Suilven	7.0	579	63
21	Breabag: Ascent from Benmore Lodge	14.0	700	65
22	Breabag: Ascent from Allt nan Uamh	12.0	670	66
23	Breabag: Link route to Conival	7.0	640	67
24	Ben More Assynt & Conival: Ascent from Inchnadamph	18.0	1112	68
25	The Oykell Horseshoe from Kinlochailsh	34.0	1448	70
26	Glas Bheinn & Beinn Uidhe: Ascent from Loch na Gainmhich	18.0	853	73
27	Glas Bheinn & Beinn Uidhe: Link route to Conival	12.0	701	76
28	Quinag: Ascent from the east	11.0	732	79
29	Quinag: Ascents from the north	10.0	700	81
30	Quinag: Ascent from Tumore	8.0	732	82
31	Quinag: Link route to Glas Bheinn	9.0	533	83

WALKING IN SCOTLAND'S FAR NORTH

Route		km	m/ascent	page
32	Beinn Leoid: Ascent from Kinloch, Loch More	15.0	1190	85
33	Beinn Leoid: Ascent from Kylestrome	27.0	853	86
34	Beinn Leoid: Ascent from Loch na Gainmhich via Eas a Chual Aluinn	24.0	1500	87
35	Beinn Leoid: Link route to Beinn Uidhe	14.0	760	90
36	Ben Stack: Ascent from Lochstack Lodge	6.0	670	93
37	Ben Hee: Ascent from West Merkland	12.0	790	95
38	Meallan Liath Coire Mhic Dhughaill: Ascent from Achfary via Lone	13.0	810	98
39	Meallan Liath Coire Mhic Dhughaill: Ascent from Aultanrynie	18.0	910	100
40	Meallan Liath Coire Mhic Dhughaill: Link route to Sabhal Beag	6.0	533	101
41	Meall Horn and the Sabhals: Ascent (all tops) from Achfary via Lone	24.0	1005	102
42	Meall Horn (direct) from Lone	13.0	792	104
43	Meall Horn: Link route to Arkle	8.0	457	104
44	Meall Horn: Link route to Foinaven	9.0	700	105
45	Arkle: Ascent from Achfary via Lone	17.0	884	106
46	Arkle: Link route to Foinaven	10.0	762	108
47	Arkle: Link Route to Meall Horn	8.0	442	108
48	Foinaven: Ascent from the north-west	13.0	869	110
49	Beinn Spionnaidh & Cranstackie: Ascent from Carbreck	11.0	985	113
50	Ben Hope: Ascent from Strath More	7.0/12.0	900	114
51	Ben Loyal: Ascent from Ribigill	13.0	762	117
52	Ben Stumanadh: Ascent from Loch Loyal	11.0	472	121
53	Ben Klibreck: Ascent from Vagastie	14.0	792	124
54	Ben Klibreck: Ascent from Altnaharra	18.0	1035	125
55	Ben Klibreck: The full traverse, from Crask Inn	34.0	1310	126
56	Morven & Scaraben: Ascent from Braemore	22.0	1280	129
57	The Assynt Horseshoe from Little Assynt	56.0	3350	131
58	A Reay Traverse from West Merkland to Gualin House	40.0	3020	135
59	Cranstackie: A long ascent from the north coast	34.0	2100	138
60	Eas a Chual Aluinn waterfall from Loch na Gainmhich	10.0	396	141
61	The Culnacraig coastal path from Blughasary	9.0	215	142
62	To Sandwood Bay (with possible extension to Cape Wrath) from Blairmore	14.0	200	143

NOTES

NOTES

NOTES

SAVE £££'s with

tgo
THE GREAT OUTDOORS

Britain's leading monthly magazine for the dedicated walker. To find out how much you can save by subscribing call

0141 302 7744

HILLWALKING • BACKPACKING • TREKKING • SCRAMBLING

Climber

IF YOU LIKE ADVENTUROUS ACTIVITIES ON MOUNTAINS OR HILLS YOU WILL ENJOY

Climber

MOUNTAINEERING / HILLWALKING / TREKKING / ROCK CLIMBING / SCRAMBLING IN BRITAIN AND ABROAD

AVAILABLE FROM NEWSAGENTS, OUTDOOR EQUIPMENT SHOPS, OR BY SUBSCRIPTION (6-12 MONTHS) from

WARNER GROUP PUBLICATIONS PLC
THE MALTINGS, WEST STREET, BOURNE, LINCS PE10 9PH
Tel: 01778 393313 Fax: 01778 394748
ISDN: 01778 423059 email: Sam.a@warners.co.uk

HIGH MOUNTAIN SPORTS &
ontheedge

....the UK's favourite climbing & mountaineering magazines

Available from Newsagents, specialist gear shops or by subscription

www.highmountainmag.com
www.ontheedgemag.com

Telford Way Ind. Est, Kettering, Northants, NN16 8UN
Tel: 01536 382563 Fax: 01536 382501
email:publishing@greenshires.com

GREENSHIRES

Get ready for take off

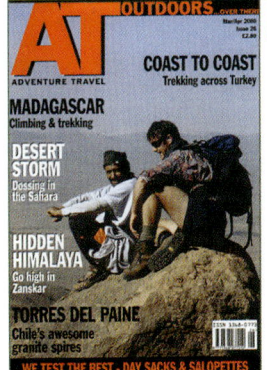

Adventure Travel helps you to go outdoors over there

More ideas, information, advice and entertaining features on overseas trekking, walking and backpacking than any other magazine - guaranteed.

Available from good newsagents or by subscription - 6 issues £15

Adventure Travel Magazine T:01789-488166

The Mountains

1. Ben Mor Coigach
2. Cul Beag
3. Stack Polly
4. Cul Mor
5. Suilven
6. Canisp
7. Braebag
8. Ben More Assynt
9. Glas Bheinn
10. Quinag
11. Beinn Leoid
12. Ben Stack
13. Ben Hee
14. Meallan Laith Coire Mhic Dhughaill
15. Meall Horn
16. Arkle
17. Foinaven
18. Cranstackie
19. Ben Hope
20. Ben Loyal
21. Beinn Stumanadh
22. Ben Klibreck
23. Morven
24. Scaraben

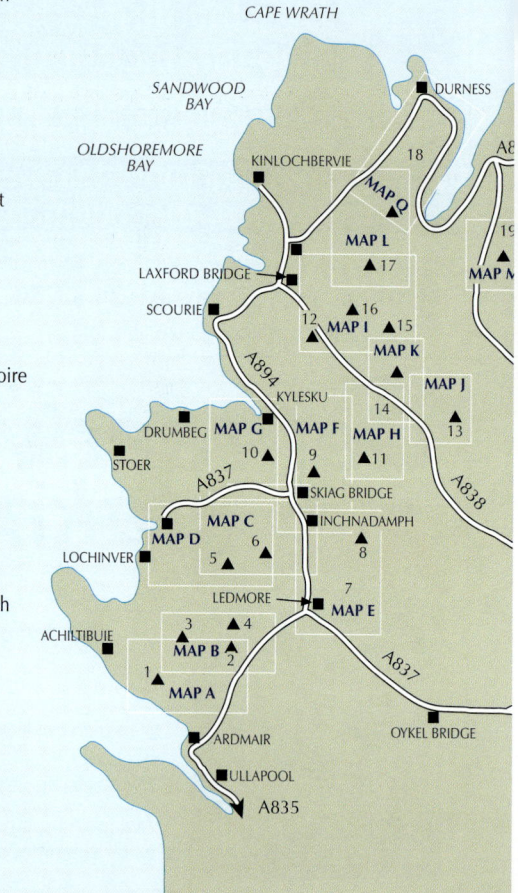

Areas covered by the guide

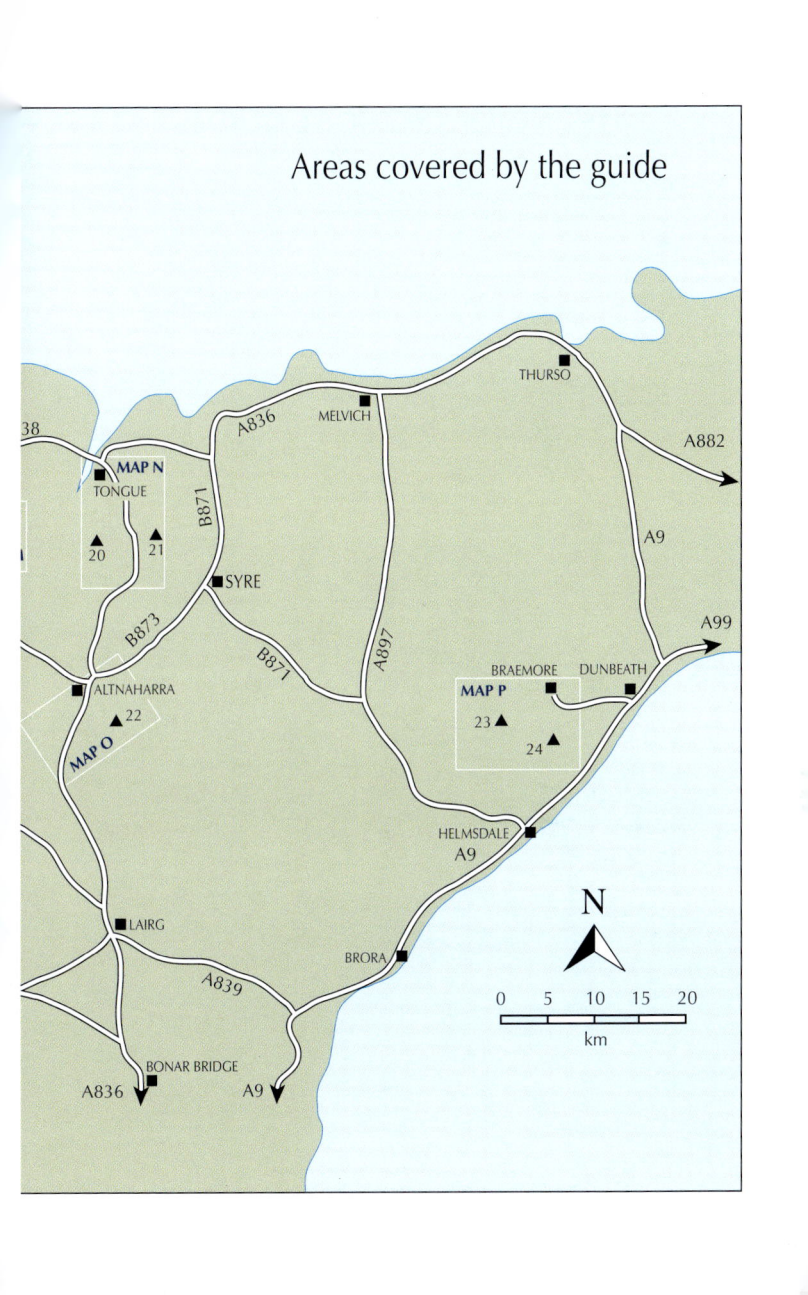

LISTING OF CICERONE GUIDES

NORTHERN ENGLAND LONG DISTANCE TRAILS
- THE DALES WAY
- THE ISLE OF MAN COASTAL PATH
- THE PENNINE WAY
- THE ALTERNATIVE COAST TO COAST
- NORTHERN COAST-TO-COAST
- THE RELATIVE HILLS OF BRITAIN
- MOUNTAINS ENGLAND & WALES
  VOL 1 WALES
  VOL 2 ENGLAND

CYCLING
- BORDER COUNTRY BIKE ROUTES
- THE CHESHIRE CYCLE WAY
- THE CUMBRIA CYCLE WAY
- THE DANUBE CYCLE WAY
- LANDS END TO JOHN O'GROATS CYCLE GUIDE
- ON THE RUFFSTUFF – 84 BIKE RIDES IN NORTH ENGLAND
- RURAL RIDES NO.1 WEST SURREY
- RURAL RIDES NO.1 EAST SURREY
- SOUTH LAKELAND CYCLE RIDES
- THE WAY OF ST JAMES LE PUY TO SANTIAGO – CYCLIST'S
- CYCLE TOURING IN SPAIN
- THE LOIRE CYCLE ROUTE

LAKE DISTRICT AND MORECAMBE BAY
- CONISTON COPPER MINES
- CUMBRIA WAY & ALLERDALE RAMBLE
- THE CHRONICLES OF MILNTHORPE
- THE EDEN WAY
- FROM FELL AND FIELD
- KENDAL – A SOCIAL HISTORY
- A LAKE DISTRICT ANGLER'S GUIDE
- LAKELAND TOWNS
- LAKELAND VILLAGES
- LAKELAND PANORAMAS
- THE LOST RESORT?
- SCRAMBLES IN THE LAKE DISTRICT
- MORE SCRAMBLES IN THE LAKE DISTRICT
- SHORT WALKS IN LAKELAND
  BOOK 1: SOUTH
  BOOK 2: NORTH
  BOOK 3: WEST
- ROCKY RAMBLER'S WILD WALKS
- RAIN OR SHINE
- ROADS AND TRACKS OF THE LAKE DISTRICT
- THE TARNS OF LAKELAND VOL 1: WEST
- THE TARNS OF LAKELAND VOL 2: EAST
- WALKING ROUND THE LAKES
- WALKS SILVERDALE/ARNSIDE
- WINTER CLIMBS IN LAKE DISTRICT

NORTH-WEST ENGLAND
- WALKING IN CHESHIRE
- FAMILY WALKS IN FOREST OF BOWLAND
- WALKING IN THE FOREST OF BOWLAND
- LANCASTER CANAL WALKS
- WALKER'S GUIDE TO LANCASTER CANAL
- CANAL WALKS VOL 1: NORTH
- WALKS FROM THE LEEDS-LIVERPOOL CANAL
- THE RIBBLE WAY
- WALKS IN RIBBLE COUNTRY
- WALKING IN LANCASHIRE
- WALKS ON THE WEST PENNINE MOORS
- WALKS IN LANCASHIRE WITCH COUNTRY
- HADRIAN'S WALL
  VOL 1 : THE WALL WALK
  VOL 2 : WALL COUNTRY WALKS

NORTH-EAST ENGLAND
- NORTH YORKS MOORS
- THE REIVER'S WAY
- THE TEESDALE WAY
- WALKING IN COUNTY DURHAM
- WALKING IN THE NORTH PENNINES
- WALKING IN NORTHUMBERLAND
- WALKING IN THE WOLDS
- WALKS IN THE NORTH YORK MOORS BOOKS 1 AND 2
- WALKS IN THE YORKSHIRE DALES BOOKS 1,2,3 AND 4
- WALKS IN DALES COUNTRY
- WATERFALL WALKS – TEESDALE & HIGH PENNINES
- THE YORKSHIRE DALES
- YORKSHIRE DALES ANGLER'S GUIDE

THE PEAK DISTRICT
- STAR FAMILY WALKS PEAK DISTRICT/STH YORKS
- HIGH PEAK WALKS
- WEEKEND WALKS IN THE PEAK DISTRICT
- WHITE PEAK WALKS
  VOL.1 NORTHERN DALES
  VOL.2 SOUTHERN DALES
- WHITE PEAK WAY
- WALKING IN PEAKLAND
- WALKING IN SHERWOOD FOREST
- WALKING IN STAFFORDSHIRE
- THE VIKING WAY

WALES AND WELSH BORDERS
- ANGLESEY COAST WALKS
- ASCENT OF SNOWDON
- THE BRECON BEACONS
- CLWYD ROCK
- HEREFORD & THE WYE VALLEY
- HILLWALKING IN SNOWDONIA
- HILLWALKING IN WALES VOL.1
- HILLWALKING IN WALES VOL.2
- LLEYN PENINSULA COASTAL PATH
- WALKING OFFA'S DYKE PATH
- THE PEMBROKESHIRE COASTAL PATH
- THE RIDGES OF SNOWDONIA
- SARN HELEN
- SCRAMBLES IN SNOWDONIA
- SEVERN WALKS
- THE SHROPSHIRE HILLS
- THE SHROPSHIRE WAY
- SPIRIT PATHS OF WALES
- WALKING DOWN THE WYE
- A WELSH COAST TO COAST WALK
- WELSH WINTER CLIMBS

THE MIDLANDS
- CANAL WALKS VOL 2: MIDLANDS
- THE COTSWOLD WAY
- COTSWOLD WALKS
  BOOK 1: NORTH
  BOOK 2: CENTRAL
  BOOK 3: SOUTH
- THE GRAND UNION CANAL WALK
- HEART OF ENGLAND WALKS
- WALKING IN OXFORDSHIRE
- WALKING IN WARWICKSHIRE
- WALKING IN WORCESTERSHIRE
- WEST MIDLANDS ROCK

SOUTH AND SOUTH-WEST ENGLAND
- WALKING IN BEDFORDSHIRE
- WALKING IN BUCKINGHAMSHIRE
- CHANNEL ISLAND WALKS
- CORNISH ROCK
- WALKING IN CORNWALL
- WALKING IN THE CHILTERNS
- WALKING ON DARTMOOR
- WALKING IN DEVON
- WALKING IN DORSET
- CANAL WALKS VOL 3: SOUTH
- EXMOOR & THE QUANTOCKS
- THE GREATER RIDGEWAY
- WALKING IN HAMPSHIRE
- THE ISLE OF WIGHT
- THE KENNET & AVON WALK
- THE LEA VALLEY WALK
- LONDON: THE DEFINITIVE WALKING GUIDE
- LONDON THEME WALKS
- THE NORTH DOWNS WAY
- THE SOUTH DOWNS WAY
- THE ISLES OF SCILLY
- THE SOUTHERN COAST TO COAST
- SOUTH WEST COAST PATH
- WALKING IN SOMERSET
- WALKING IN SUSSEX
- THE THAMES PATH
- TWO MOORS WAY
- WALKS IN KENT BOOK 1
- WALKS IN KENT BOOK 2
- THE WEALDWAY & VANGUARD WAY

SCOTLAND
- WALKING IN THE ISLE OF ARRAN
- THE BORDER COUNTRY – A WALKERS GUIDE
- BORDER COUNTRY CYCLE ROUTES
- BORDER PUBS & INNS – A WALKERS' GUIDE
- CAIRNGORMS, WINTER CLIMBS 5TH EDITION
- CENTRAL HIGHLANDS 6 LONG DISTANCE WALKS
- WALKING THE GALLOWAY HILLS
- WALKING IN THE HEBRIDES
- NORTH TO THE CAPE
- THE ISLAND OF RHUM

- THE ISLE OF SKYE – A WALKER'S GUIDE
- WALKS IN THE LAMMERMUIRS
- WALKING IN THE LOWTHER HILLS
- THE SCOTTISH GLENS SERIES
  1 – CAIRNGORM GLENS
  2 – ATHOLL GLENS
  3 – GLENS OF RANNOCH
  4 – GLENS OF TROSSACH
  5 – GLENS OF ARGYLL
  6 – THE GREAT GLEN
  7 – THE ANGUS GLENS
  8 – KNOYDART TO MORVERN
  9 – THE GLENS OF ROSS-SHIRE
- SCOTTISH RAILWAY WALKS
- SCRAMBLES IN LOCHABER
- SCRAMBLES IN SKYE
- SKI TOURING IN SCOTLAND
- THE SPEYSIDE WAY
- TORRIDON – A WALKER'S GUIDE
- WALKS FROM THE WEST HIGHLAND RAILWAY
- THE WEST HIGHLAND WAY
- WINTER CLIMBS NEVIS & GLENCOE

IRELAND
- IRISH COASTAL WALKS
- THE IRISH COAST TO COAST
- THE MOUNTAINS OF IRELAND

WALKING AND TREKKING IN THE ALPS
- WALKING IN THE ALPS
- 100 HUT WALKS IN THE ALPS
- CHAMONIX TO ZERMATT
- GRAND TOUR OF MONTE ROSA VOL. 1 AND VOL. 2
- TOUR OF MONT BLANC

FRANCE, BELGIUM AND LUXEMBOURG
- WALKING IN THE ARDENNES
- ROCK CLIMBS BELGIUM & LUX.
- THE BRITTANY COASTAL PATH
- CHAMONIX - MONT BLANC WALKING GUIDE
- WALKING IN THE CEVENNES
- CORSICAN HIGH LEVEL ROUTE: GR20
- THE ECRINS NATIONAL PARK
- WALKING THE FRENCH ALPS: GR5
- WALKING THE FRENCH GORGES
- FRENCH ROCK
- WALKING IN THE HAUTE SAVOIE
- WALKING IN THE LANGUEDOC
- TOUR OF THE OISANS: GR54
- WALKING IN PROVENCE
- THE PYRENEAN TRAIL: GR10
- THE TOUR OF THE QUEYRAS
- ROBERT LOUIS STEVENSON TRAIL
- WALKING IN TARENTAISE & BEAUFORTAIN ALPS
- ROCK CLIMBS IN THE VERDON
- TOUR OF THE VANOISE
- WALKS IN VOLCANO COUNTRY
- SNOWSHOEING MONT BLANC/WESTERN ALPS
- VANOISE SKI TOURING
- ALPINE SKI MOUNTAINEERING
  VOL 1: WESTERN ALPS
  VOL 2: EASTERN ALPS

FRANCE/SPAIN
- ROCK CLIMBS IN THE PYRENEES
- WALKS & CLIMBS IN THE PYRENEES
- THE WAY OF ST JAMES
  VOL 1 AND VOL 2 – WALKER'S
- THE WAY OF ST JAMES
  LE PUY TO SANTIAGO – CYCLIST'S

SPAIN AND PORTUGAL
- WALKING IN THE ALGARVE
- ANDALUSIAN ROCK CLIMBS
- BIRDWATCHING IN MALLORCA
- COSTA BLANCA ROCK
- COSTA BLANCA WALKS VOL 1
- COSTA BLANCA WALKS VOL 2
- WALKING IN MALLORCA
- ROCK CLIMBS IN MAJORCA, IBIZA & TENERIFE
- WALKING IN MADEIRA
- THE MOUNTAINS OF CENTRAL SPAIN
- THE SPANISH PYRENEES GR11 2ND EDITION
- WALKING IN THE SIERRA NEVADA
- WALKS & CLIMBS IN THE PICOS DE EUROPA
- VIA DE LA PLATA
- WALKING IN THE CANARY ISLANDS VOL 1: WEST AND VOL 2: EAST

SWITZERLAND
- ALPINE PASS ROUTE, SWITZERLAND
- THE BERNESE ALPS A WALKING GUIDE
- CENTRAL SWITZERLAND
- THE JURA: HIGH ROUTE & SKI TRAVERSES
- WALKING IN TICINO, SWITZERLAND
- THE VALAIS, SWITZERLAND – A WALKING GUIDE

GERMANY, AUSTRIA AND EASTERN EUROPE
- MOUNTAIN WALKING IN AUSTRIA
- WALKING IN THE BAVARIAN ALPS
- WALKING IN THE BLACK FOREST
- THE DANUBE CYCLE WAY
- GERMANY'S ROMANTIC ROAD
- WALKING IN THE HARZ MOUNTAINS
- KING LUDWIG WAY
- KLETTERSTEIG NORTHERN LIMESTONE ALPS
- WALKING THE RIVER RHINE TRAIL
- THE MOUNTAINS OF ROMANIA
- WALKING IN THE SALZKAMMERGUT
- HUT-TO-HUT IN THE STUBAI ALPS
- THE HIGH TATRAS
- WALKING IN HUNGARY

SCANDINAVIA
- WALKING IN NORWAY
- ST OLAV'S WAY

ITALY AND SLOVENIA
- ALTA VIA – HIGH LEVEL WALKS DOLOMITES
- CENTRAL APENNINES OF ITALY
- WALKING CENTRAL ITALIAN ALPS
- WALKING IN THE DOLOMITES
- SHORTER WALKS IN THE DOLOMITES
- WALKING ITALY'S GRAN PARADISO
- LONG DISTANCE WALKS IN ITALY'S GRAN PARADISO
- ITALIAN ROCK
- WALKS IN THE JULIAN ALPS
- WALKING IN SICILY
- WALKING IN TUSCANY
- VIA FERRATA SCRAMBLES IN THE DOLOMITES
- VIA FERRATAS OF THE ITALIAN DOLOMITES
  VOL 1: NORTH, CENTRAL AND EAST
  VOL 2: SOUTHERN DOLOMITES, BRENTA AND LAKE GARDA

OTHER MEDITERRANEAN COUNTRIES
- THE ATLAS MOUNTAINS
- WALKING IN CYPRUS
- CRETE – THE WHITE MOUNTAINS
- THE MOUNTAINS OF GREECE
- JORDAN – WALKS, TREKS, CAVES ETC.
- THE MOUNTAINS OF TURKEY
- TREKS & CLIMBS WADI RUM JORDAN
- CLIMBS & TREKS IN THE ALA DAG
- WALKING IN PALESTINE

HIMALAYA
- ADVENTURE TREKS IN NEPAL
- ANNAPURNA – A TREKKER'S GUIDE
- EVEREST – A TREKKER'S GUIDE
- GARHWAL & KUMAON – A TREKKER'S GUIDE
- KANGCHENJUNGA – A TREKKER'S GUIDE
- LANGTANG, GOSAINKUND & HELAMBU TREKKERS GUIDE
- MANASLU – A TREKKER'S GUIDE

OTHER COUNTRIES
- MOUNTAIN WALKING IN AFRICA – KENYA
- OZ ROCK – AUSTRALIAN CRAGS
- WALKING IN BRITISH COLUMBIA
- TREKKING IN THE CAUCASUS
- GRAND CANYON & AMERICAN SOUTH WEST
- ROCK CLIMBS IN HONG KONG
- ADVENTURE TREKS WEST NORTH AMERICA
- CLASSIC TRAMPS IN NEW ZEALAND

TECHNIQUES AND EDUCATION
- OUTDOOR PHOTOGRAPHY
- SNOW & ICE TECHNIQUES
- ROPE TECHNIQUES
- THE BOOK OF THE BIVVY
- THE HILLWALKER'S MANUAL
- THE TREKKER'S HANDBOOK
- THE ADVENTURE ALTERNATIVE
- BEYOND ADVENTURE
- FAR HORIZONS – ADVENTURE TRAVEL FOR ALL
- MOUNTAIN WEATHER

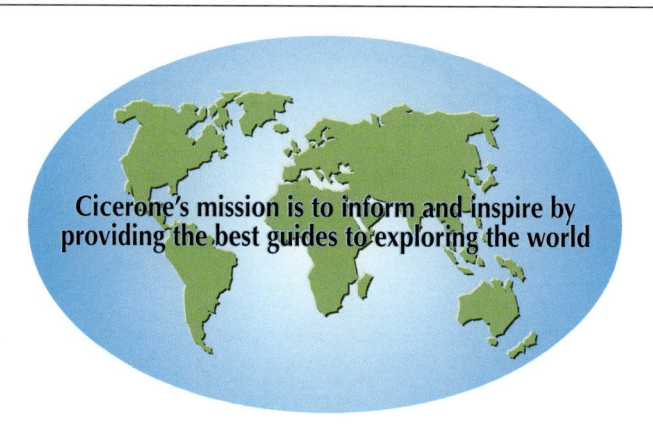

Cicerone's mission is to inform and inspire by providing the best guides to exploring the world

Since its foundation over 30 years ago, Cicerone has specialised in publishing guidebooks and has built a reputation for quality and reliability. It now publishes nearly 300 guides to the major destinations for outdoor enthusiasts, including Europe, UK and the rest of the world.

Written by leading and committed specialists, Cicerone guides are recognised as the most authoritative. They are full of information, maps and illustrations so that the user can plan and complete a successful and safe trip or expedition – be it a long face climb, a walk over Lakeland fells, an alpine traverse, a Himalayan trek or a ramble in the countryside.

With a thorough introduction to assist planning, clear diagrams, maps and colour photographs to illustrate the terrain and route, and accurate and detailed text, Cicerone guides are designed for ease of use and access to the information.

If the facts on the ground change, or there is any aspect of a guide that you think we can improve, we are always delighted to hear from you.

Cicerone Press
2 Police Square Milnthorpe Cumbria LA7 7PY
Tel:01539 562 069   Fax:01539 563 417
e-mail:info@cicerone.co.uk   web:www.cicerone.co.uk

CICERONE